Arthur Asa Berger, PhD

Vietnam Tourism

"**D**rawing upon Professor Berger's background and experience in cultural studies, *Vietnam Tourism* offers an imaginative and personal portrayal of Vietnam as a tourism destination. In a fresh and innovative manner, the book combines a subjective diary style with a systematic reflection of Vietnam as an idea. The idea includes a pre-trip dimension (Virtual Vietnam), a during-trip component (Semiotic Vietnam), and a post-trip reflection (Remembering Vietnam). A very welcome addition to the field of destination studies."

Professor Brian King, PhD
Head, School of Hospitality,
Tourism, and Marketing,
Victoria University,
Australia

Vietnam Tourism

Vietnam Tourism

Arthur Asa Berger, PhD

THHP

The Haworth Hospitality Press®
An Imprint of The Haworth Press, Inc.
New York • London • Oxford

For more information on this book or to order, visit
http://www.haworthpress.com/store/product.asp?sku=5275

or call 1-800-HAWORTH (800-429-6784) in the United States and Canada
or (607) 722-5857 outside the United States and Canada

or contact orders@HaworthPress.com

Published by

The Haworth Hospitality Press®, an imprint of The Haworth Press, Inc., 10 Alice Street,
Binghamton, NY 13904-1580.

All photos of Vietnam by Julie Adams.

Cover design by Jennifer M. Gaska.

Cover photos by Julie Adams.

Library of Congress Cataloging-in-Publication Data

Berger, Arthur Asa, 1933-
    Vietnam Tourism / Arthur Asa Berger.
        p. cm.
    Includes bibliographical references and index.
    ISBN 0-7890-2570-1 (hard : alk. paper) — ISBN 0-7890-2571-X (soft : alk. paper)
    1. Tourism—Vietnam. I. Title.

G155.V5B37 2005
338.4'791597—dc22
                                                                    2004020217

CONTENTS

ABOUT THE AUTHOR

Arthur Asa Berger is Professor Emeritus of Broadcast and Electronic Communication Arts at San Francisco State University, where he taught from 1965 to 2002. He also taught at the University of Milan in 1963-1964 as a Fulbright Scholar and at the Heinrich Heine University in Dusseldorf in 2001 as a Fulbright Senior Specialist. He received his BA in literature and philosophy from the University of Massachusetts and his MA in journalism from the University of Iowa, where he also attended the Writers' Workshop. He received his PhD in American studies from the University of Minnesota, where he wrote his dissertation on Al Capp's satirical comic strip, *Li'l Abner*.

He is the author of 50 books on popular culture, media, humor, and everyday life and has published more than 100 articles in various journals. His books have been translated into German, Swedish, Italian, Korean, Chinese, and Turkish. He has lectured in a dozen countries during the course of his career. Berger is also an artist and has illustrated a number of his books, as well as books by others. Among his books are *Media Analysis Techniques*; *Essentials of Mass Communication Theory*; *Bloom's Morning: Coffee, Comforters and the Secret Meaning of Everyday Life*; *Ads, Fads and Consumer Culture*; *An Anatomy of Humor*; *Ocean Travel and Cruising: A Cultural Analysis*, and three mysteries that also function as textbooks: *Postmortem for a Postmodernist*; *The Mass Comm Murders: Five Media Theorists Self-Destruct*; and *Durkheim Is Dead: Sherlock Holmes Is Introduced to Social Theory*. Dr. Berger is married to Phyllis Wolfson, who taught philosophy at Diablo Valley College until her recent retirement. They have two children and two grandchildren. He lives in Mill Valley, California, and can be reached by e-mail at aberger@ sfsu.edu.

Why is travel so exciting? Partly because it triggers the thrill of escape, from the constriction of the daily, the job, the boss, the parents. "A great part of the pleasure of travel," says Freud, "lies in the fulfillment of . . . early wishes to escape the family and especially the father." The escape is also from the traveler's domestic identity, and among strangers a new sense of selfhood can be tried on, like a costume. The anthropologist Claude Lévi-Strauss notes that a traveler takes a journey not just in space and time (most travel being to places more ancient than the traveler's home) but "in the social hierarchy as well"; and he has noticed repeatedly that arriving in a new place, he has suddenly become rich (travelers to Mexico, China, or India will know the feeling). The traveler's escape, at least since the Industrial Age, has also been from the ugliness and racket of Western cities, and from factories, parking lots, boring turnpikes, and roadside squalor.

Paul Fussell (Ed.)
The Norton Book of Travel

Foreword

Vietnam is a tourist's paradise, and I believe that it is the best travel destination in the world today. The country is a magical mix of natural, cultural, and historical delights that appeals to emerging new travelers who seek more than the usual replication of their own culture in a far-off land. Straddling the edge of Southeast Asia, Vietnam demarcates the edge of the Indochina peninsula as it abuts the Pacific Ocean from the South China Sea to the Gulf of Tonkin. The country's lengthy coastline, which stretches from the Mekong Delta in the south to the Red River Delta in the north, contains beautiful beaches and a range of other coastal landforms. The lowland plains are covered in a rich tapestry of green rice paddies, and inland the country rises to include cooler plateaus and forested mountains. Three-quarters of the country are either hilly or mountainous, forming the borders with Laos and Cambodia.

People—nearly 80 million of them, and growing—are everywhere. Today it is the thirteenth most populated country in the world, yet, as with all travel, a beautiful land and wonderful climate mean little for the tourist unless the host nation is friendly and willing to embrace visitors. The Vietnamese people excel at hospitality; visitors are greeted by warm smiles, friendly hosts, and an interest in where they come from and what they are doing in the country. Then there is the food. Although established as a firm favorite across the globe, this is the source and it is good! One of the main delights in visiting the country is sampling its outstanding cuisine. *Com* (rice) and *pho* (noodle soup) are the staple foods and these are complemented by chicken, beef, pork, and seafood. Vegetables and fruits are widely available. The Vietnamese bread, a legacy from the French, is wonderful.

Add to the land and the people the complex history and the unique culture of the country, and Vietnam looms large on the horizon of must-see nations. Thus it is extremely timely that Arthur Berger has written this extraordinary book that combines a unique blend of travelog and insightful commentary on a nation in transition. He writes with the authority of a leading global scholar but manages to present stunning word pictures of Vietnam, conjuring images that simply leap off the page. An accomplished wordsmith, Berger's writing takes the reader straight to the core of the land and its people, giving it a sense of place in our hearts and minds. He delivers a wealth of information while adding a smorgasbord of insights, providing the reader with a multitude of vignettes of everyday life in this historic land.

Berger's book is unique in its ethnographic approach, through which he tries to understand the deeper significance of the sights and experiences. This can be likened to a major leap forward in travel books as Berger deconstructs his perceptions and experiences of Vietnam to give greater meaning to the country as a tourist destination. He does this through the four approaches of analyzing, imagining, interpreting, and reflecting on the country. For the reader trying to understand Vietnam in a more meaningful manner than merely glancing over the glossy brochures and slick guidebooks, Berger delivers a wonderful portrayal of the richness, intensity, and diversity of life available to be observed by a tourist.

This work stands apart from nearly all other travel books that I have read. The author presents a travel guide and travel book. Scholarly commentary on the country is woven throughout the pages, combined with insightful views on Vietnam and its place in history and the world. Arthur Berger manages to energize the traditional tourism discourse, enhancing the written word by integrating his pretour, tour, and posttour thoughts and experiences by his comparison of the virtual and actual Vietnam.

This book is sensational. The reader will thoroughly enjoy it and also will ruminate over it long afterward.

Ross K. Dowling, PhD
Foundation Professor of Tourism
Edith Cowan University
Australia

Preface

Vietnam is a long, thin, vaguely "S"-shaped country that hugs the eastern coast of the Indochina peninsula, clutching tightly to Laos and Cambodia, as if it were afraid it might suddenly fall off into the South China Sea. Only thirty miles wide at its narrowest point, with major rice-producing areas in the north and south, it is a long, thin country somewhat reminiscent of Chile, with Chile's pencil-thin shape.

Vietnam has four major cities—Hanoi, with approximately 1.5 million inhabitants, Haiphong, with around 1 million, Da Nang with 350,000 in the central area, and the gigantic conurbation of Ho Chi Minh City, in reality a province, with somewhere between 6 and 8 million inhabitants covering an enormous geographical area. The rest of the cities are much smaller.

With nearly 80 million people, half of whom are under thirty, Vietnam is the thirteenth most populated country in the world and also has one of the youngest populations. Curiously, except for the Vietnam War, as people in the United States called it (the Vietnamese call it the American War), and news stories about atrocities committed during the war that appear in news headlines occasionally, one reads relatively little about Vietnam in the American press. Generally, only during times of natural disaster or a trade dispute do we hear about Vietnam.

It is as if Americans, in a collective act of willful repression, have forced the country out of their minds, perhaps because the television images of it, and hence our memories, are so terrible.

So it is a great surprise, when you visit the country, to find that it is full of gentle, friendly people. The Vietnamese generally like Americans and, although our military was driven out many years ago, we still have a considerable presence there in the form of dollar bills, which are a parallel currency to the Vietnamese dong.

The Vietnamese are an incredibly hardworking people and although they are poor by Western standards, they seem to be spirited and happy. A richness and delicacy is found in their culture, a lightness and joyfulness that is quite wonderful. And their food is simply fabulous. Vietnam is a seductive country. You travel to the country not knowing what to expect—perhaps afraid due to the descriptions in guidebooks of terrible diseases and dangerous characters lurking in the cities.

The seduction begins with the beautiful landscapes. The rice fields, with each stalk of rice planted in a perfect line with the others in its row, and in line with all the other rows, are remarkable. In the fields you often can hear farmers directing their water buffalo—stop, go right, go left—and the water buffalo, patient beasts who otherwise would be lounging around in muddy water, do as they are told. In the northwest, around Sapa, the terraced rice paddies snake up almost to the top of enormous hills. You can only marvel at them as you consider the backbreaking work that was necessary to make the terraces, which extend as far as the eye can see into the distance.

Halong Bay, an incredibly beautiful place with limestone islets, is a United Nations Educational, Scientific, and Cultural Organization (UNESCO) World Heritage site. Seeing the sun set in Halong Bay, watching the islands fade into the darkness, is a marvelous experience. Gorgeous beaches line the 3,600-kilometer coast, and in the lotusland of the Mekong Delta, the brown rivers, streams, and canals, bordered by towering palm trees, flow everywhere.

Many cities, including Hanoi, have tree-lined boulevards and areas where many of the buildings, with their French architecture, make you think for a moment that you might be in the south of France. The Vietnamese were fortunate that the French occupied the country during a period when French architects designed elegant, graceful buildings.

As I have mentioned, Vietnamese food is quite remarkable; it has a lightness and delicacy that is surprising. It is not just a variation of Chinese food, although the Chinese, who occupied Vietnam for 1,000 years, obviously influenced Vietnamese culture and cuisine. The national dish, *pho* (pronounced "fur," as in the French word for fire), originated in Hanoi and spread downward. It is one of the main icons of Vietnamese culture and a diet staple. I'll have more to say about *pho* later.

Although Vietnam is many thousands of years old, it is important to remember that it has existed as a unified country only since July 1976, so it is a young nation in that respect. How it will evolve, or what place it will hold in the world community even ten years from now, is difficult to know.

Having traveled from the top to the bottom of the country, having visited cities from Sapa in the far northwest to Chau Doc and Can Tho in the Mekong Delta, I can't help but wonder what Vietnam will be like in the future. It is impossible to predict. I'm sure, however, that Vietnam ten or twenty years from now will still hold many remarkable surprises, just as Vietnam now surprises and generally delights the tourists who come to visit it. The question I ask myself, as I think about Vietnam's future, is—will it lose its magic? Will Vietnam lose its innocence, its playfulness, and its charm, and become just one more country that has become overwhelmed by its tourists (and hardened and commercialized by them)? The Vietnamese also think and worry about this question.

From this book I believe you will gain some insight and information regarding the rapidly developing tourism industry in Vietnam. In addition, you will learn about tourism in the country through my experiences there. I played two roles in Vietnam: In one respect, I was a typical sightseeing tourist, but in another respect, I was an observer, an ethnographer trying to understand the deeper significance of the various activities I participated in and elements I saw, so I could offer an interpretation of Vietnamese everyday life and culture. Tourists are in search of that which is different; I suggest that seeing Vietnamese everyday life and the ways in which it differs from life in other countries is an important aspect of tourism in Vietnam.

Acknowledgments

I thank Professor Kaye Chon for his assistance in publishing this book. I also express my appreciation to the staff at The Haworth Press—the copy editor, the production editor, the marketing staff, and everyone else—for the wonderful work they did in publishing my book.

I also owe a special debt of gratitude to Julie Adams, who provided the beautiful images of Vietnam that are reproduced in this book. I met Julie at breakfast one morning in the Salute Hotel in Hanoi. When I learned that she is a photographer, I contacted her when this book was accepted for publication. She's been absolutely wonderful to work with.

Finally, let me express my gratitude to the people of Vietnam, who received my wife and me into their beautiful country with such graciousness and hospitality, and who made our visit to their country a truly memorable experience.

Modernity first appears to everyone as it did to Lévi-Strauss, as disorganized fragments, alienating, wasteful, violent, superficial, unplanned, unstable and inauthentic. On second examination, however, this appearance seems almost a mask, for beneath the disorderly exterior, modern society hides a firm resolve to establish itself on a worldwide base.

Modern values are transcending the old divisions between the Communist East and the Capitalist West and between the "developed" and "third" worlds. The progress of modernity ("modernization") depends on its very sense of instability and inauthenticity. For moderns, reality and authenticity are thought to be elsewhere: in other historical periods and other cultures, in purer, simpler lifestyles. In other words, the concerns of moderns for "naturalness," their nostalgia and their search for authenticity are not merely casual and somewhat decadent, though harmless, attachments to the souvenirs of destroyed cultures and dead epochs. They are also components of the conquering spirit of modernity—the grounds of its unifying consciousness.

The central thesis of this book holds the empirical and ideological expansion of modern society to be intimately linked in diverse ways to modern mass leisure, especially to international tourism and sightseeing.

Dean MacCannell,
*The Tourist: A New Theory
of the Leisure Class*

Introduction

Let me begin by saying something about one of the methodologies I employed in writing several parts of this book—a research technique known as ethnography. This methodology attempts to capture the nature of everyday life in whatever place it is being employed.

A NOTE ON ETHNOGRAPHY

Ethnography is a form of research, based on participant observation, in which the experiences of the investigator play an important role in the analysis of whatever is being studied. Literally, the word ethnography means "a picture of a people or a nation" ("ethnos" means people or nation and "graphy" means picture). The great anthropologist Claude Lévi-Strauss offers an insight into ethnography in his classic work *Tristes Tropiques* (1970). He writes:

> It may seem strange that I should so long have remained deaf to a message which had after all been transmitted for me ever since I first began to read philosophy, by the masters of the French school of sociology. The revelation did not come to me, as a matter of fact, till 1933 or 1934 when I came upon a book which was already by no means new: Robert H. Lowie's *Primitive Society*. But instead of notions borrowed from books and at once metamorphosed into philosophical concepts I was confronted with an account of first-hand experience. The observer, moreover, had been so committed as to keep intact the full meaning of his experience. (pp. 62-63)

This book combines my firsthand experiences in Vietnam and my speculations about the meanings of these experiences with research into writings by scholars and journalists about Vietnam.

1

THE DESIGN OF THE BOOK

This study of tourism in Vietnam is divided into four parts. Part I is analytical and deals with Vietnam as a tourist destination; it contains statistics about tourism in Vietnam and material on the problems Vietnam faces as it struggles to develop its tourism industry as well as a discussion of the various experiences that Vietnam offers as a tourist destination.

Part II of the book is a combination ethnography and travelog, which deals with my experiences in planning to visit Vietnam and activities I did when I was there. It also discusses the way Vietnam is represented in tourism guidebooks and what travel writers say about Vietnam and its people.

In Part III, I offer a socio-semiotic interpretation of Vietnamese commonplace objects (*pho,* conical straw hats, spring rolls, pith helmets, dong) and important Vietnamese sites the typical tourist will visit (Ho Chi Minh Museum, Hanoi, the Cu Chi Tunnels, the Mekong Delta, Ho Chi Minh City). This part of the book considers what is distinctive, or "authentic," about Vietnam. It deals with what the great anthropologist Bronislaw Malinowski described as the "imponderabilia" of everyday life in Vietnam and interprets various objects, artifacts, heroes, and places that give Vietnam its distinctive character as a tourist destination. Roland Barthes, the French cultural analyst and semiotician, would have called it "Vietnamese-ness." I'll say more about his work later.

In Part IV, I offer a meditation on my experiences in Vietnam and some speculations about the globalization of tourist industry and about differences between American and Vietnamese culture. As you can see from this description, a good deal of this book is based on personal experiences and interpretations of observations, which is true of all ethnographies.

WHY PEOPLE BECOME TOURISTS: USES AND GRATIFICATIONS

Why do so many people travel? What is the lure that makes so many people wander about the world? It costs money to travel and tourists often face difficulties and sometimes even dangerous hazards. So what has led tourism to become one of the most important sectors in the world market?

Some possible answers to this question are taken from social science research on media use. One commonly studied aspect of the media is its effects on people. This considers such matters as the role the media plays in politics, in our consumer culture, in influencing some children and adolescents to act out violently, and so on. However, a long and important tradition of media study focuses attention on the uses and gratifications that the media provides audiences.

Data on uses and gratifications were obtained by social scientists who asked people questions such as why they watch certain television programs or what they like about soap operas. I have compiled a list of some of the more important uses and gratifications mentioned by respondents and will adapt these to an understanding of the motivations of tourists who visit Vietnam.

The matter of motivations is complicated and will be explored later in a discussion of consumer cultures and individual volition. Tourists might decide how and where to travel based on certain group affiliations and not on their psychological profiles.

The following are possible reasons for traveling to Vietnam:

1. *To experience the beautiful.* One of the most important features of tourism in Vietnam (and, of course, certain other countries as well) is its striking beauty, which is often mentioned in travel literature, and was verified by tourists I met during my travels there. They generally told me that they had heard that Vietnam was scenic, but were still unprepared for its remarkable beauty. Personally speaking, I found my time in Halong Bay and the Mekong Delta to be truly transforming and transcendent experiences, and I'm sure I'm not alone in feeling this way about these places.

2. *To participate in history.* People long to connect themselves to events and places of historical significance. That is, they want to find ways to "participate" in history. A visit to Vietnam helps tourists "connect" with one of the major wars of recent years and with Vietnam's epic struggle for independence. Americans, of course, would find Vietnam of considerable importance because the Vietnam War was such an important part of our history. The *Viet Kieu,* or Vietnamese living abroad, who return to

Vietnam (and often bring their children to see where they were born and grew up) also have this as an important motivation. Many Americans first saw Vietnam when they watched news programs that dealt with the Vietnam War on television; some of them want to see the country for themselves.

3. *To be amused and entertained.* Tourism is a form of consumption. Tourists are seeking experiences that they hope will enrich their lives and recharge their depleted (by the routines of everyday life) batteries. For many tourists, Vietnam's wonderful beaches are an important reason for their visits. Others are intrigued by Vietnam's large cities with their historically important buildings, nightlife, and other inducements. Generally speaking, tourists want to get an overview of a new culture and have experiences that cover a number of "must-see" touristic bases.

4. *To obtain an outlet for sexual drives in a guilt-free manner.* Sexual tourism has a major presence in the tourism industries of many countries. Visitors to foreign lands often do not feel constrained by the psychological and moral burdens put on them in their native lands. Many of these tourists see Vietnamese women (and men as well) as willing partners about whom they can feel guilt-free when engaging in sexual relations. In some countries, and Vietnam is one of them, sexual tourism is very well developed and a major part of the tourism industry. However, officials in such countries seem to be trying to curtail it, in part because of the spread of AIDS.

5. *To help gain an identity.* One benefit tourism offers to people is to help them cast off their everyday or regular identities—that is, the ones they have in their native lands—and take on (if only for a while) the new identities of traveler, adventurer, explorer, fat cat, and so on. Tourists from highly developed countries find themselves, relatively speaking, rich in Vietnam, where the average annual income is less than $400 a year, where good hotels cost only $20 a night, and an excellent meal costs just a few dollars. This momentary casting off of an old identity and assumption of a new one can have lingering effects upon these tourists; it can provide them with a sense of possibility they may never have realized before.

6. *To satisfy curiosity.* Human beings are naturally curious. Tourism provides a means for people to satisfy their curiosity about

how people in other lands live, what they eat, how they dress, what they believe in, and any number of other matters. In a sense, tourists are amateur cultural anthropologists and ethnologists, whose experiences are driven in large part by their curiosity about human diversity. In Vietnam this diversity exists on many different levels, from the ordinary life of Vietnamese in their towns and cities to the various members of the hill tribes, who can be seen only in certain cities.

Gratifications provided by tourism such as the ones just described help explain the emotional aspects of why so many people currently travel, and why people have traveled throughout history.

PART I:
VIETNAM AS A TOURIST
DESTINATION—
AN ANALYTIC PERSPECTIVE

Rice fields, with their regularly spaced rows, are some of the most beautiful and most typical sights in Vietnam.

Chapter 1

The Pros and Cons of Vietnam Tourism

STATISTICS ON TOURISM IN VIETNAM, THAILAND, AND CAMBODIA

Although tourism has been increasing in Vietnam over the past decade, especially compared to its neighbor Thailand and to many countries in Western Europe, Vietnam still has relatively few tourists. In this section, the development of tourism in Vietnam and in its neighboring countries of Thailand and Cambodia are addressed. The problems Vietnam faces in developing its tourism industry and the positives of visiting Vietnam as its tourism industry evolves are considered.

The following list shows that tourism has been growing rapidly in Vietnam in recent years. It lists the number of visitors to Vietnam (rounded off to the nearest thousand) per year. In the course of only three years, from 1999 to 2002, tourism increased by almost 1 million visitors (see <www.vietnamtourism.com>). (We cannot be certain of the accuracy of these statistics, I should add.)

1999	1,781,000
2000	2,140,000
2001	2,330,000
2002	2,627,000

It is useful to compare Vietnam with Thailand, where tourism is much more highly developed. The following figures are for Thailand during the same years (rounded off to the nearest thousand).

1999	8,580,000
2000	9,578,000
2001	10,132,000
2002	10,872,000

Thailand has approximately four times as many visitors as Vietnam (see <www2.tat.or.th/stat/web/static_index.php>). On the other hand, in 2002, Cambodia had only 466,000 visitors, so it lags well behind Vietnam and Thailand as a tourist venue, even though it has one of the greatest tourist attractions in the world, Angkor Wat (see <www. embassy.org/cambodia.tourismbrief.html>).

Although it is increasing, tourism to Asia still is much less developed than tourism in Europe and other countries, such as Canada and Mexico. The following list details the number of tourists and population for the year 2001 of some major tourist destinations and for Thailand and Vietnam (see <www.world-tourism.org/facts/trends/destination.htm>).

Country	Number of Visitors	Population
France	75.2 million	58 million
Spain	50.1 million	40 million
United States	44.9 million	270 million
Italy	39.0 million	57 million
China	33.2 million	1280 million
United Kingdom	22.8 million	58 million
Mexico	19.8 million	100 million
Austria	18.2 million	8 million
Thailand	10.1 million	61 million
Vietnam	2.3 million	77 million

Clearly, tourism in Vietnam, even though it is growing rapidly, still is less well developed than tourism in many other countries. These figures also suggest that the possibilities of tourism increasing rapidly in Vietnam are considerable; Vietnam hopes to attract as many as 9 million tourists by the year 2010.

VISITORS IN VIETNAM BY COUNTRY IN 2001

The following list shows the "top ten" countries that sent visitors to Vietnam in 2001 and offers the number of visitors (rounded off to the nearest thousand). These figures do not distinguish between tourists and business travelers (see <www.vietnamtourism.com/e_pages/tourist/ general/sltk_kQ5Thang2002.htm>).

Country of Origin	Number of Visitors
China	672,000
United States	230,000
Taiwan	200,000
Japan	152,000
France	99,000
Australia	84,000
Cambodia	76,000
Korea	75,000
United Kingdom	64,000
Laos	40,000
Germany	39,000

China leads, as might be expected, because it borders Vietnam and has many commercial relationships with it. China is followed by the United States, which has recently developed commercial relationships with Vietnam. Also, many *Viet Kieu* return to visit friends and introduce their country of origin to their children. France also sends many tourists to Vietnam, which can be explained in part by France's historical relationship with Vietnam.

According to statistics found on the Web site of the World Tourism Organization (WTO), the United Kingdom, Germany, France, Japan, and the United States rank in the order listed in terms of amounts of money spent on tourism, so it is reasonable to expect to find tourists from these countries in many different lands (Berger, 2004, pp. 58-59).

Country	Expenditure	Population	Per Capita	Ranking
United States	60 billion	270 million	$202	5
Germany	46 billion	80 million	$575	2
United Kingdom	37 billion	59 million	$637	1
France	17 billion	58 million	$293	3
Japan	31 billion	120 million	$258	4

Residents of the United Kingdom, on a per capita basis, are the great tourists of the world, followed closely by Germany. People from the United States spend approximately $60 billion dollars a year on tourism, but because there are approximately 270 million of them, it works out to around $202 per person. Residents of the United Kingdom spend approximately $37 billion dollars a year on tourism, but the smaller population (59 million) results in a figure of approximately $637 per capita.

Tourism is an enormous industry. As Eric J. Leed writes in *The Mind of the Traveler: From Gilgamesh to Global Tourism* (1991):

> Travel, in the form of tourism, is becoming increasingly pervasive in our world. By the turn of the millennium, it will be the most important sector of world trade, surpassing oil, and is currently the second largest retail industry in the United States. The impression of the commonality of travel is intensified when one includes in the ranks of travelers those who obviously belong but do not appear in tourism statistics—business travelers, nomads, commuters, itinerant laborers, refugees, members of the armed services, diplomatic personnel, temporary and permanent immigrants. (pp. 1-2)

When you add these kinds of travelers together, you can understand why tourism is such a large industry. Leed's book was written in 1991, and since then mass tourism has become even more highly developed.

SOME PROBLEMS OF VIETNAM'S TOURISM INDUSTRY

Vietnam faces a number of difficulties as a popular tourist destination. The following sections list and briefly discuss some of them. The focus here is on how typical mainstream (middle-class and middle-aged) Americans and other tourists who are contemplating travel to Southeast Asia tend to perceive Vietnam.

Lack of Infrastructure

In a sense, for mainstream tourism to flourish in a country, everything must be in place at the same time. By this I mean a country must have good roads, a well-developed transportation system (air and train), well-staffed tourism companies, and quality hotels, in addition to sites of interest. Countries without a well-developed infrastructure can attract some tourists—adventurous types, people with special interests, and backpackers (who don't spend much money and therefore aren't as coveted as middle-class tourists), but not mainstream tourists in large numbers.

Vietnam's railroad system is very primitive and many trains don't travel at more than twenty or thirty miles per hour. The roads in some places are in very poor condition. However, government officials in Vietnam are aware of the importance of tourism and now are making rapid progress in developing its infrastructure and in training people to work in the tourism industry.

Connie Mok and Terry Lam (1998) list some of the difficulties the Vietnam tourism industry faces: "There are a number of constraints hindering Vietnam's tourism development. They include the poor infrastructure, lax legal systems, graft, the lack of accommodation facilities of international standards, and inadequate skilled workers and qualified management people" (<http://www.hotel-online.com/Trends/ JournalTravelTourismMarketing/HotelDevelopmentVietnam_Nov1997. html>). Since this article was written, Vietnam seems to have made progress in developing its tourism industry and is now educating a considerable number of students majoring in tourism, building hotels, and developing sites of touristic interest.

General Fear of Third World Countries

Vietnam is generally seen as a very poor country and many tourists are afraid that in a third world, or underdeveloped, country they will not be able to find suitable hotels, that adequate medical facilities won't be available, that they will be besieged by beggars, that they face personal risk of robbery, that they won't be able to buy things they need, and that they will encounter numerous other difficulties, such as wide-scale flooding after rainstorms. In this respect, of course, Vietnam is no different from many other third world countries, where personal safety is a continual problem. The following discussion of the material in guidebooks regarding the dangers of travel in Vietnam demonstrates this anxiety in rather graphic images.

Ignorance Regarding Vietnam

Many "problems" just discussed are due to faulty information people receive about Vietnam, its culture, and its attractions. It may be a third world country, but it also has excellent tourism companies and many wonderful sites—from Halong Bay and Hue to beautiful beaches. Vietnam has been rapidly building hotels in important tourist sites and now offers hotels of all kinds—from super-luxurious ones to middle-range, three-star hotels, down to very primitive hotels. In some areas, such as Ho Chi Minh City, hotels are found in abundance; in other cities, hotels are scarce.

Vietnam War Memories and Images

Many Americans only know that the United States had a terrible war and suffered its only major military defeat in Vietnam. Often, all potential tourists know is what they see in occasional television documentaries, films, and travel pieces and news reports about events in Vietnam. It is quite likely that most people still perceive Vietnam as a war-ravaged country, full of destroyed buildings and half-starved people. The images of the post–Vietnam War era still linger. Films, such as *The Quiet American* (2002), create images in people's minds of Vietnam that may be appealing but also may create certain fears and anxieties about life there.

The Political Regime

Vietnam is one of the few remaining communist countries, though the Vietnamese communists have, in reality, embraced capitalism with its *Doi Moi* policy (economic decentralization and liberalization), and vistors don't get the sense that the people are oppressed by a cruel dictatorship. The Vietnamese people seem to be able to lead their lives more or less as they wish. Nevertheless, for some Americans the idea of visiting a communist country where so many American soldiers died creates problems.

Competition from Thailand

Vietnam faces major competition from a very well-developed tourism industry in Thailand, which attracts large numbers of tourists and has many exotic sites to rival those of Vietnam. Thailand is seen as "safe" and easily visited, unlike Vietnam, about which many tourists who seek middle-class comforts have certain anxieties. You don't need a visa to travel to Thailand, either. Although obtaining a $65-visa might seem to be a trivial matter, many tourists are deterred by such inconveniences and prefer to travel instead to countries where tourist visas are not required.

BENEFITS OF VIETNAM
AS A TOURIST DESTINATION

Vietnam has many attractions that make it a desirable country to visit. A number of them are considered here.

Vietnam Is Exotic

When deciding where to travel, tourists search for venues that are different from their everyday experiences—what might be called "the exotic." In this respect Vietnam is a powerful lure, for its culture is quite exotic by American standards. Its culture, foods, street life, natural sites, and the various hill tribes in their traditional costumes all function as oppositions to the ordinary or traditional everyday life of an American (or person from any first world country, for that matter).

From 1883 to 1955, Vietnam was ruled by the French and as a postcolonial nation, its past is reflected in its architecture and food, such as the wonderful baguettes and excellent soups. This means that although Vietnam can be described as exotic, it is not too exotic for the average tourist. In a sense, then, Vietnam represents the best of both worlds—the exotic, tinged in various ways by French (that is, modern) civilization. In contrast, Thailand can be seen as too commercial, too developed, and in some areas of the country too inauthentic for many tourists.

Vietnamese Cuisine Is Superb

Vietnamese food, which incorporates elements of Chinese, French, Indian, and other cuisines but maintains its own identity, is considered one of the great cuisines of the world. Therefore, food is a great attraction for tourists and many excellent restaurants are scattered throughout Vietnam, some of which are quite modest in ambience and inexpensive. A central element of Vietnamese cuisine, which distinguishes it from other cuisines, is its reliance on fish sauce. This will be discussed later. Lonely Planet, a guidebook publisher, devotes an entire book to the Vietnamese cuisine, which is alleged to include some 500 dishes. Some Vietnamese beers also are quite excellent.

Adventure Possibilities

As I read over notes I took during our Vietnamese trip, I noticed that my wife and I had surprising and wonderful experiences every day—every day some new delight, every day something remarkable to remember, every day something unexpected, fascinating, and interesting. For tourists who are looking for an escape from ordinary, everyday life routines, Vietnam's somewhat primitive nature, its lack of sophistication, is of great importance.

Vietnam has authenticity, a primary goal of many tourists who continually search for real experiences in contrast to staged and planned ones in many tourist sites, what might be called touristic theater. In Vietnam, the feeling pervades that one is an explorer and adventurer rather than a tourist, so Vietnam's semideveloped infrastructure serves to heighten a sense in tourists that their experiences are authentic.

You feel that you are seeing ordinary life there, life as it really is lived. This sense of adventure is a powerful source of Vietnam's tourist appeal. It is still possible, of course, to live in the "tourist bubble" and stay in five-star hotels, eat in five-star restaurants, and maintain one's accustomed level of comfort and distance, but it is more difficult in Vietnam (once you get out of the major cities) than in many other countries. Tourists generally want to avoid "tourist traps" full of artificial and staged events. Vietnam doesn't have many tourist traps.

Some scholars have argued that this quest for authenticity no longer means much in our postmodern world, and that in a postmodern world in which simulations are the norm, tourists only care about having fun and being entertained, and don't care whether their experiences in foreign lands are "real" or staged and "artificial." I would disagree with this contention and argue that tourists still seek authenticity of life in foreign lands, as a contrast to their everyday lives.

Many tourists, I would argue, go to Vietnam to escape the postmodernized, and in many respects unsatisfying, highly developed countries in which many of them live.

Vietnam's Physical Beauty

As I mentioned earlier, many tourists are surprised by the remarkable beauty of Vietnam, with its lush landscapes in many shades of green, by its spectacular Halong Bay, by its dramatic hill areas, and by the Mekong Delta. This is important because tourists want to "see" a country, and a country such as Vietnam, which is so attractive and has so many "photo opportunities," is a country well-suited to satisfy the tourist's need to "gaze" and take photographs. Many tourists are in search of transcendental experiences, of ways of transforming themselves, and Vietnam's spectacular landscapes and seascapes provide many possibilities for such transformation.

The Friendliness of the Vietnamese People

Perhaps because Vietnam hasn't been overrun by tourists, the Vietnamese people are remarkably friendly toward Americans or people from other countries involved in the Vietnam War. The Vietnamese people have put the war behind them (even if the American people have not) and are very hospitable. This friendliness and gentleness may be connected to their religious beliefs and their culture.

In countries where a great deal of tourism exists, such as France, it is not unusual for tourists to detect a certain amount of hostility on the part of natives, some of whom seem to feel that they are being overrun by foreigners and who seem to have become tired of having to answer questions. Friendliness is tied partly to national character, and the Vietnamese national character is generally an open and friendly one.

Returning American Soldiers and Vietnamese from America (Viet Kieu)

Quite a few tours in Vietnam are specially designed for returning American soldiers, who wish to revisit some sites of battles in which they may have participated and want to see what Vietnam is like decades after they left the country. Veterans can visit the Cu Chi Tunnels, hundreds of miles of which were dug by Vietnamese soldiers, and take a boat trip (in small boats) to see where the Viet Cong generals hid from the Americans and planned their battles.

In addition, many Vietnamese who long ago fled Vietnam return, often with their children, to show them their home country and to see friends and relatives. The number of returning Vietnamese from America and other countries is expected to grow considerably over the years. Some *Viet Kieu,* who left Vietnam when the communists took over, are returning to Vietnam permentantly.

Sites of Historical and Natural Interest

Vietnam is a new nation but an old country with a history dating back more than 4,000 years. Ancient sites, such as My Son, the Cham settlement just north of Hoi An, and other buildings of historical interest are worth seeing, such as those in Hue. Buildings from the French colonial period and others related to the Vietnam War also are interesting sites.

Halong Bay, several hours by bus south of Hanoi, is a UNESCO World Heritage Site and is a popular attraction, as are the miles and miles of beaches in Vietnam, which has a 3,000-kilometer coastline facing the South China Sea.

Where to Go

Particular highlights which any visitor to Vietnam would do well not to miss are: (from north to south) the hill station of Sapa for its stunning scenery and hill-tribes . . . Hanoi, which itself is historical, beautiful and cultured, lies at the heart of a vast range of architectural and scenic treasures (which can be done on day trips out); time permitting, Cat Ba Island and Halong Bay should be included for their coastal scenery. Moving south there then follows a yawning gulf of mediocrity so it is not until Hué that the next stop should be made. Hué's palaces and mausoleums deserve two days but most visitors give them only one (it does rather depend on the weather). The splendid train journey for Hué to Danang should not be missed but Danang itself has little to commend it (apart from the Cham Museum) which is why most travellers head straight for nearby Hoi An, an enchanting 17th century mercantile town. Between here and Saigon the seaside town of Nha Trang is the main attraction but the sleepy resort of Phan Thiet should be considered as a more tranquil alternative. Saigon, although a city of six million, is really a small town: no sensible person will stray far from the colonial core which, containing as it does all anyone could possibly need in the way of hedonistic pleasures (and with scarcely any intellectual or cultural distractions) is the most popular destination in the country. The six million are jammed into suburbs; an indescribable density of bodies live out their days in an inferno of noise, sewage, and motorbikes. While the Mekong Delta has its attractions, it would be hard to justify its inclusion on the "must-see" list. (Colet and Eliot, 1999, p. 19)

It's instructive to consider where tours go in Vietnam. The average country tour tends to visit certain sites that are commonly agreed upon as important. The following list includes places that people visit who take the Overseas Adventure Travel tour of Vietnam. This particular tour is featured because I recently received a brochure from this company describing its tour to Vietnam. People on this tour spend a few days in Thailand and twelve nights in Vietnam. It costs $1,890 for sixteen days, including airfare. Because it costs at least $1,000 to fly to all the places on the tour (including two internal flights in Vietnam, which cost approximately $160) and it includes most meals, it is a relatively inexpensive tour.

Hanoi
    Visit Old Quarter
    Ho Chi Minh house
    Temple of Literature
    Museum of Ethnology
    Hanoi Hilton (Hoa Lo Prison)
    Water puppet show
    Halong Bay
Da Nang
    Cham Museum
    My Son (Champa Ruins)
Hue
    Citadel
    Antiques museum

Tu Duc tombs
Sail on Perfume River
Ho Chi Minh City (Saigon)
Cathedral
Post Office
Site of former U.S. Embassy
Cu Chi
Cu Chi Tunnels
Mekong Delta cruise

This list of places to go and things to do is typical; many tours of Vietnam visit the same sites and offer the same activites. Thus, for example, large numbers of tourists in Saigon take day trips to see the Cu Chi Tunnels; in many cases these day trips also visit the remarkable Cao Dai Cathedral, which this tour skips for some reason.

Chapter 2

The Consumer Culture and Vietnam

TOURISM AND CONSUMER CULTURES: THE GRID-GROUP TYPOLOGY

Being a tourist costs money. Tourism, whatever else it might involve, is a kind of consumption and plays an important role in our contemporary global consumer culture. The term "consumer culture" is something of an oversimplification. Some scholars suggest that there are four different consumer cultures and that these consumer cultures are connected to certain beliefs and values held in common by their members. The discussion that follows deals with the ideas of the British social anthropologist Mary Douglas (1997) and the American political scientists Michael Thompson, Richard Ellis, and Aaron Wildavsky, authors of *Cultural Theory* (1990).

In *Cultural Theory,* Douglas's grid-group typology is used to deal with sociological theory and political cultures, but it also has implications that will be of some use to us in our analysis of taste preferences by tourists. Thompson, Ellis, and Wildavsky explain the classification system that Douglas developed, the grid-group typology, as follows:

> She argues that the variability of an individual's involvement in social life can be adequately captured by two dimensions of sociality: group and grid. *Group* refers to the extent to which an individual is incorporated into bounded units. The greater the incorporation, the more individual choice is subject to group determination. *Grid* denotes the degree to which an individual's life is circumscribed by externally imposed prescriptions. The more binding and extensive the scope of the prescriptions, the less of life that is open to individual negotiation. (p. 5)

Douglas's "group" dimension involves the extent to which an individual's life is shaped and sustained by membership in a group. Her "grid" dimension involves whether an individual in a group has to obey relatively few or many rules and prescriptions.

The authors assert that grid-group relationships generate five, and only five, different lifestyles or ways of life, described by Wildavsky in an earlier work as political cultures (Berger, 1989). These are: hierarchy, egalitarianism, individualism, fatalism, and autonomy. Autonomy has few adherents and is based on withdrawing from society; it is of little concern to us here. So, for all practical purposes, only four political or consumer cultures exist.

Wildavsky, who for many years was a professor at the University of California at Berkeley, offered a slightly different explanation of grid-group theory (which is the basis for cultural theory), one that may help us understand it better. Cultural theory, Wildavsky argued, helps people answer two fundamental questions. The first involves cultural identity *(Who am I?)* and the second involves behavior *(What should I do?).* Wildavsky (in Berger, 1989) explains:

> The question of identity may be answered by saying that individuals belong to a strong group, a collective that makes decisions binding on all members or that their ties to others are weak in that their choices bind only themselves. The question of action is answered by responding that the individual is subject to many or few prescriptions, a free spirit or tightly constrained. The strength or weakness of group boundaries and the numerous or few, varied or similar prescriptions binding or freeing individuals are the components of their culture. (p. 25)

This implies, then, that four political cultures (though he, too, later added a fifth that is of no concern to us) arise from the answers to these two questions. Wildavsky describes these four cultures as hierarchical, individualist, egalitarian, and fatalist.

These cultures are formed by the strength and weakness of group boundaries and by the numbers and kinds of rules and prescription. As Wildavsky writes:

> Strong groups with numerous prescriptions that vary with social roles combine to form hierarchical collectivism. Strong groups whose members follow few prescriptions form an egalitarian culture, a shared life of voluntary consent without coercion or

inequality. Competitive individualism joins few prescriptions with weak group boundaries, thereby encouraging ever new combinations. When groups are weak and prescriptions strong—so that decisions are made for them by people on the outside—the controlled culture is fatalistic. (Berger, 1989, p. 25)

Wildavsky changed the names of some of his four cultures as his theory matured, but the four just listed are representative of his ideas. Sometimes he used the term *hierarchical elitists* and in other cases *elitists* rather than *hierarchical collectivists,* because he thought that description might be a bit confusing.

We must keep one point in mind: In any democratic society, according to Wildavsky, *only* four political cultures are possible. He argued that individuals make political decisions based on their allegiance to one of these four groups and not on self-interest, because people usually can't determine what is in their own self-interest. The same applies to consumer cultures.

The following list shows the four consumer cultures. Members of these four political cultures or consumer cultures generally don't identify themselves as members of one of these groups and often aren't even aware of their existence. Individuals simply have certain core values and beliefs that place them in one of these four cultures.

Culture	Group Boundaries	Number of Prescriptions
Hierarchists/elitists	strong	numerous and varied
Egalitarians/enclavists	strong	few and weak
Individualists	weak	few and weak
Fatalists/isolates	weak	numerous and varied

Mary Douglas (1997), who collaborated with Wildavsky on a number of projects, used the terms consumer cultures and lifestyles instead of political cultures, and replaced the term "fatalists" with *isolates* and "egalitarians" with *enclavists.* She suggests that it is their membership in one of the four consumer cultures or lifestyles, each of which is in conflict or, as she puts it, "agonistic," with the three others, that explains people's consumer choices. They may not be able to explain their beliefs and values that place them in one of the four consumer cultures, but they recognize that they don't belong to the other three consumer cultures.

CONSUMER CULTURES AND TOURIST CHOICES

Consumption choices, Douglas and Wildavsky argue, are culturally determined and not based on individual wants or desires. When we think about tourism, then, grid-group cultural theory suggests that tourist choices also are culturally determined rather than a matter of individual choice; of course, people planning to take tours aren't always cognizant of this fact. Individuals make choices, but their choices are ultimately guided by their membership in a consumer culture and antagonism toward other consumer cultures.

As Douglas explains in her essay "In Defense of Shopping" (in Falk and Campbell, 1997), our consumer choices are guided, in part, by hostility toward other groups. She writes:

> None of these four lifestyles (individualist, hierarchical, enclavist, isolated) is new to students of consumer behavior. What may be new and unacceptable is the point that that these are the only four distinctive lifestyles to be taken into account, and the other point, that each is set up in competition with the others. Mutual hostility is the force that accounts for their stability. These four distinct lifestyles persist because they rest on incompatible organizational principles. Each culture is a way of organizing; each is predatory on the others for time and space and resources. It is hard for them to co-exist peacefully, and yet they must, for the survival of each is the guarantee of the survival of the others. Hostility keeps them going. (p. 19)

Douglas offers her theory to counter theories about consumption that are derived from a framework based on individualist psychology. She claims that "cultural alignment is the strongest predictor of preferences in a wide variety of fields" (Falk and Campbell, 1997, p. 23).

This implies that choices tourists make about where to go and what kind of experience to pursue are based on two powerful forces: their desire to *avoid* people in other consumer cultures and *to be with* people who are in their own consumer cultures. A logic exists behind the kind of tours people take as well as other forms of consumption. Members of the four consumer cultures may have similar incomes, but the way they travel is, Douglas suggests, ultimately shaped by their cultural alignment—that is, their membership in one of the four consumer cultures.

Douglas concludes with a radical suggestion; she states that the idea that shopping is the expression of individual wants is not correct, for this individualistic view doesn't take into account the matter of cultural bias. As Douglas points out in the conclusion to her essay (Falk and Campbell, 1997):

> The idea of consumer sovereignty in economic theory will be honoured in market research because it will be abundantly clear that the shopper sets the trends, and that new technology and new prices are adjuncts to achieving the shopper's goal. The shopper is not expecting to develop a personal identity by choice of commodities; that would be too difficult. *Shopping is agonistic, a struggle to define not what one is but what one is not* [italics added]. When we include not one cultural bias, but four, and when we allow that each is bringing critiques against the others, and when we see that the shopper is adopting postures of cultural defiance, then it all makes sense. (p. 30)

If she is correct, and four different and mutually antagonistic lifestyles or consumer cultures exist, then the various kinds of tours people take, the places they go, and the modes of travel they use are tied to their membership in one consumer culture and rejection of the others.

Consumer choices are, then, a means of cultural defiance. This means it isn't socioeconomic class and discretionary income that shape travel and tourism decisions, but lifestyles or memberships in one of Douglas's four consumer cultures, and, of particular importance, a desire to distance oneself from members of the other consumer cultures.

TRAVEL PREFERENCES IN VIETNAM AND CULTURAL ALIGNMENTS

Members of each of the four antagonistic but mutually dependent cultures, according to this theory, seek out different kinds of experiences when they travel and for ways to be with people like themselves. Assuming Douglas is correct about the role of lifestyles and consumer cultures in travel decision making, let me suggest how people in each of the different consumer cultures might travel.

When they travel, elitists search for hierarchy and social distance from other consumer cultures and lifestyles, which they obtain by selecting luxury cruises or other expensive kinds of travel. There they can assume that, due to the cost of the travel and the kind of people who travel this way, they will be with people similar to themselves. Individualists, on the other hand, don't want anyone to tell them what to do and tend to travel independently, booking their hotels and other aspects of their trips through their travel agents or on their own, using the Internet. They generally are not the kind of people to take packaged tours.

Egalitarians will be eco-tourists and take tours that focus on cultural experiences and nature preservation, wanting to do whatever they can to preserve nature. They will want to show their connections with people everywhere and will tend to avoid tourism enjoyed by elitists and individualists. Fatalists (or isolates), who are generally the least wealthy and have few resources, will take trips by automobile or bus, or choose short excursions.

One major reason that tourists find certain travel experiences unpleasurable is that they mistakenly chose the wrong kind of tour or travel arrangements. They might have ended up, grid-group theory explains, with people from an antagonistic consumer culture.

The theories and analysis of Wildavsky and Douglas suggest that we should reconsider conventional hypotheses about travel and tourism as a form of consumption made by many scholars. Their views, focusing on individualistic psychology, do not recognize the importance of the different consumer cultures and may be overly simplistic and inadequate. If we want to understand why people choose to travel the way they do and to where they decide to travel, we shouldn't probe their minds and psyches but determine the consumer culture to which they belong.

A question arises: What kind of tourists go to Vietnam and what kinds of tours do they take? Based on the theories of Wildavsky and Douglas, the following are possibilities.

Elitists	Visit coastal cities while on ocean cruises
Individualists	Take individually designed tours
Egalitarians	Take set-departure group tours and nature tours
Fatalists	Backpacking and cheap hotels

Elitists would visit Vietnam while on ocean cruises along the coast, because the lack of five-star hotels and paucity of amenities such as golf courses might make them want to avoid the difficulties inherent in traveling in Vietnam. Individualists would arrange for private tours, which they could design with the help of travel agents, and would provide maximum flexibility. Egalitarians would tend to take set-departure group tours and nature tours to Vietnam to show their solidarity with the Vietnamese people and to do what they can to preserve the natural beauty of the country. Fatalists would travel on their own, by bus, and stay in inexpensive hotels. They would approximate the backpacker lifestyle.

These suggestions are all hypothetical because, despite the power of group affiliations, people are different and some members of one consumer culture may behave differently from the way the theories of Wildavsky and Douglas predict. In addition, people sometimes switch from one political culture or lifestyle to another, so any choices a person makes about travel in Vietnam may reflect either solidarity with a given group and political culture or a movement toward a different one.

ABOUT IMAGINING, INTERPRETING, AND REMEMBERING VIETNAM

With this, the comparative statistical portrait of tourism in Vietnam and theoretical analysis of tourism, in general, comes to a conclusion. In the next part of the book I offer a combination ethnography and tourism analysis that deals with how people contemplating tours to Vietnam are led to "see" the country—what I describe as a form of imagining Vietnam or as "Virtual Vietnam," by books on the country by travelers and by guidebooks of Vietnam. The material in the next part of the book focuses upon my experiences in imagining Vietnam before I went there. I would suggest that my experiences are typical of those any tourist might encounter in preparing to visit a country such as Vietnam. In the third part of the book I offer a semiotic analysis of Vietnamese "signs" and deal with a number of objects (material culture), individuals, and places that give the country its unique character and authenticity—what might be described as the vernacular or everyday Vietnam.

PART II:
VIRTUAL VIETNAM—
IMAGINING VIETNAM

For a relatively small country, Vietnam has immense geographical and cultural diversity. Its varied climate and landscape range from the four seasons of the mountainous north to the year-round tropical temperatures of the lush south.

Vietnam's cultural diversity stems from its intriguing history dating back more than 4,000 years. Its historical legacy includes a thousand years of Chinese occupation, which has left a very strong cultural influence evident in the pagodas, local cuisine and continuing practice of Confucianism. The Cham civilization, which blossomed in the central region until the fourteenth century, has left many ancient Hindu-like temples. Vietnam's regal past can still be seen in the former capital of Hue and its Citadel and Royal Tombs. The French colonial period is still evident in many parts of Vietnam, as illustrated by the distinctive yellow pastel-colored architecture of its villas and administrative buildings.

In Vietnam you can find unspoiled beaches along the coastline stretching 3,200 km north to south and mountainous regions where minority peoples continue to live isolated from the modern world. Pastoral landscapes of lush rice paddies and fresh vegetation offer ample opportunities to observe the rural lifestyle of eight percent of Vietnam's population. Today, most of the country remains relatively unchanged, although in major cities you will discover a cosmopolitan atmosphere with modern infrastructure.

Buffalo Tours Brochure, Vietnam

The Ho Chi Minh Mausoleum, constructed from 1973-1975, is one of the biggest tourist attractions in Hanoi. Located in Ba Dinh Square, it houses the remains of Vietnam's former president and was built over the area on which "Uncle Ho" chaired national meetings.

Chapter 3

Vietnam: Image and Reality

I intended to write a book on Vietnam before I visited the country, and so I wrote much of the material in this part of the book, which deals with what I would describe as my "imagined" Vietnam, when I was in the process of planning my trip. As you might expect, the difference between the image I had of Vietnam before I went there and the reality of Vietnam was quite substantial. Generally speaking, people planning tours to a foreign country purchase guidebooks and read other literature about that country. These books, along with sources such as magazine and newspaper articles (generally with photographs) and television programs, provide tourists with an "image" of the country they will be visiting, an image that often is quite distorted. The following is what I wrote before I went to Vietnam.

VIETNAM AS AN IMAGINED PLACE

For the moment, Vietnam is just a place that I've imagined. I know it exists, but for me it is a virtual land, distant and mysterious and yet, because I'll be going there soon, somehow part of my life. My image of it is based on articles and books, films, photographs, and television footage, much of which has been horrendous. I had heard that Vietnam is what Thailand used to be like thirty years ago, before it became Westernized and more of a consumer culture. A friend of mine told me it was a wonderful place. It struck me, then, that Vietnam would be an interesting country to visit, as a kind of opposite pole to America. I wanted to travel there and observe its everyday life and popular culture, two topics that I've done research on and written about over the past forty years. I would arrive as a tourist, and that would color my experiences there.

PICO IYER'S PICTURE OF SAIGON AND HANOI

I knew a good deal about Vietnam before I went there. Or, at least, I thought I did. I recall how Pico Iyer's (1993) description of Vietnam (in his book *Falling Off the Map: Some Lonely Places of the World*) affected me. It made me curious about the country. His descriptions of the legions of Vietnamese on motorbikes brought back memories of Thailand; in Bangkok and Chiang Mai, and most other cities I've visited in Thailand, motorbikes, motorcycles, *tuk-tuks,* and motorized vehicles of all kinds had an overwhelming presence.

They were like army ants, on a rampage. You had to watch out for them all the time, and every step you took was fraught with danger. Crossing a street, at times, took on the quality of being a death-defying act. This matter, which I term "hyper-motorbike-ization" poses a problem for those involved in tourism but also gives tourists a sense of excitement in dealing with the threat, both psychological (provoking anxiety) and physical, that all these motorbikes pose to tourists.

Iyer writes in his chapter "Yesterday Once More" about Saigon, which now is officially called Ho Chi Minh City:

[T]he only word for Saigon is "wild." One evening I counted more than a hundred two-wheel vehicles racing past me in the space of sixty seconds, speeding round the jam-packed streets as if on some crazy merry-go-round, a mad carnival without a ringmaster. I walked into a dance club and found myself in the midst of a crowded floor of hip gay boys in sleeveless T-shirts doing the latest moves to David Byrne; outside again, I was back inside the generic Asian swirl, walking through tunnels of whispers and hisses. "You want boom-boom?" "Souvenir for your dah-ling?" "Why you not take special massage?" Shortly before midnight, the taxi girls stream out of their nightclubs in their party dresses and park their scooters outside the hotels along "Simultaneous Uprising" Street. Inside, Indian and Malaysian and Japanese trade-fair delegates huddle in clusters circling like excited schoolboys and checking out the mini-skirted wares, while out on the street legless beggars hop about, and crippled girls offer oral services, and boys of every stripe mutter bargains for their sisters. (1993, pp. 134, 135)

Iyer's description of Saigon is remarkable for its detail and sense of excitement. You get the sense, from his words, that Saigon is just throbbing with energy and a fabulous, out-of-this-world—that is, really wild—kind of place. You don't get the sense that Saigon, from his description of the city, is a lonely place that has somehow fallen off the map.

His evocation of Hanoi is equally graphic and suggests the power of globalization and the mass media, a subject he deals with in a book he wrote several years later on that subject:

> Everywhere seems a marketplace in Hanoi, and every street is bubbling over with free trade: one block given over to a stack of black-and-white TVs, one to a rack of bicycles. In another block, thirty barbers were lined up, with their backs to traffic, their mirrors set along the wall before them. Old men puffed Hero and Gallantes cigarettes over pyramids of Nescafe bottles, bookshops exploded with stacks of Madonna fan mags, copies of *Ba Tuoc Mongto Crixto* (and, of course, piles of TOEFL Preparation Books). In the covered market, fifteen-dollar a kilo turtles and fat snakes sat next to MARADONA JEANS caps and shirts with ONE HUNDRED DOLLARS on them. And out on the streets, the stalls were loaded with knockoff Casios, Disney T-shirts, Hong Kong watches, Chinese fans, Snoopy bags, flashing clocks, and pills guaranteed to save one from "addiction to narcotics." (1993, pp. 122, 123)

In researching the country, I also purchased and read several guidebooks on Vietnam—*Lonely Planet Vietnam* (Florence and Storey, 1999), *The Rough Guide to Vietnam* (Dodd and Lewis, 2000), and several others. In bookstores and libraries I looked at other books about Vietnam, many with photographs. So the region is a collection of images in my mind's eye, as well as a hodgepodge of descriptions and maps which locate important cities, hotels, and restaurants.

TWO WRITERS ON THE VIETNAMESE PASSION FOR FOOD

One book I read was Susan Brownmiller's *Seeing Vietnam: Encounters of the Road and Heart* (1994), which describes a trip she made with a photographer friend through Vietnam. She was on assignment and got special treatment from the Vietnamese authorities. Brownmiller made use of a number of scholarly sources, and her discussion of the Vietnamese obsession with food is quite striking. She writes:

> Pressed for a cultural stereotype, I'd say that the Vietnamese are a nation of serious, sensual, and prideful eaters. . . . A diner who appreciates the subtle wonders of Vietnamese cuisine can't help but acquire a gut-level understanding of Vietnamese history. Over the centuries gastronomic contributions from several conquering nations were orchestrated by local cooks into a distinct and original gestalt. Early and frequent invasions by China brought in stir-fry cooking along with bean curd, rice noodles, and chopsticks. A lengthy and honorable Buddhist vegetarian tradition encouraged the inventive use of fresh greens, shoots and sprouts, and contrasting textures. A beef-eater's Mongolian hot-pot traditions probably originated during the thirteenth-century invasion by Kublai Khan. In addition to leaving Vietnamese cooks with the culinary secrets of caramelized sauces and crusty baked bread, the French added white potatoes, tomatoes, and asparagus to the vegetable patch and the local cuisine. . . . Finally, there's the absolute freshness of the food. This watery land of lakes and rivers bordering the Gulf of Tonkin and the South China Sea is blessed with an abundance of fish and crustaceans. (pp. 49, 50)

I was struck by Brownmiller's fascination with the Vietnamese cuisine, but I can understand it, because the food in Vietnam is supposed to be so wonderful.

Andrew X. Pham's *Catfish and Mandala: A Two-Wheeled Voyage Through the Landscape and Memory of Vietnam* (1999), was much different. Pham, a *Viet Kieu* (foreign Vietnamese), escaped with his family and arrived in the United States in 1977. He went back some twenty years later and records his experiences cycling through Vietnam, with flashbacks to his family's experiences during the war. It is a very personal book and reveals a great deal about Vietnamese culture.

Pham agrees with Brownmiller about the importance of eating in Vietnam. He writes:

One by one the breakfast women weave through the alleys. The parade of food baskets ribbons the morning air with the varied aromas from every region of Vietnam: *bank canh* (udon in chicken broth), *bun bo hue* (spicy beef and anchovy-paste noodle soup), *hu tieu* (Chinese-style noodle soup), *banh beo* (rice dumpling with shrimp powder and fish sauce), *tau hu* (soft tofu with ginger syrup), *banh cuon* (rice crepes with Vietnamese sausage and fishsauce), *soi* (sweet rice with mung beans and coconut shavings), *banh mi thit* (ham-and-pickled-daikon sandwiches), and a host of other morning food. Vietnam is a country of food, a country of skinny people obsessed with eating. (pp. 122-123)

These citations make me think that when I get there I should pay a great deal of attention to the importance of food in everyday Vietnamese life. I've always been interested in food's relation to cultural concerns. I'd written articles on McDonald's hamburgers in the United States, on Wimpy's hamburgers in the United Kingdom, and had "deconstructed" the classic American breakfast of orange juice, cereal and milk, bacon and eggs with pan-fried potatoes, coffee and cream, and toast.

I've read that Vietnam has one of the great cuisines of the world. It seems that an emperor, centuries ago, demanded fifty different dishes with each meal, so the Vietnamese have a cuisine with 500 different dishes and a long history of concern, if not obsession, with food.

I also read Claire Ellis's *Culture Shock! A Guide to Customs and Etiquette* (2000), which seems to be designed for businesspeople going to Vietnam for extended periods. It has a good deal of useful information about Vietnamese etiquette, food, customs, and beliefs. Although information provided in guidebooks tends to overlap, they are all useful in their own ways.

THE VIETNAM WAR

I was moved by Harrison Salisbury's *Behind the Lines: Hanoi* (1967), which is a record of a stay he had in Hanoi between December 23, 1966, and January 7, 1967. His book brought back memories of those terrible days, when our television news programs were full of "body counts" and propaganda about how well the war was going.

Among the attractive architecture of Vietnam, one will occasionally see the shell of a destroyed building. Surrounded by beauty, these remnants serve as visible reminders of the Vietnam War.

The book is a rather compelling description of the havoc the United States military wreaked upon Hanoi and surrounding areas via the bombardments from American aircraft. It also portrays the incredible resiliency of the North Vietnamese, who repaired railroad lines and bridges almost immediately after they had been damaged or destroyed by bombs. Salisbury points out that he was treated very well and that the Vietnamese didn't hold him or most Americans responsible for the war—only President Lyndon Johnson and his advisors.

Salisbury offers a graphic portrait of the effects of the bombings in his discussion of his visit to Namdinh, once the third-largest city in North Vietnam. He writes:

> We drove about Namdinh, through the textile area, and stopped in Silk Street. For blocks and blocks I could see nothing but desolation. Residential housing, stores, all the buildings were destroyed, damaged or abandoned. I felt that I was walking

through the city of a vanished civilization. Here and there a handful of young men and women were at work, patiently pulling down lumber from broken houses and neatly stacking it. Many of the streets were so devastated that no one could live in them. Others had simply been abandoned in the wholesale evacuation. (p. 100)

At the end of this chapter Salisbury wonders "whether, in the end, the heaviest price might not be that paid by us Americans for our stubborn pursuit of a military theory which seemed to have little connection with reality" (p. 103).

Most common food items can be found at local markets—from fruits and vegetables to fresh poultry and other staples.

Chapter 4

Touring Vietnam in Safety and Comfort

LOGISTICS

It is one thing to decide to visit Vietnam; it is another to figure out what to do once you are there. It was easy for me to find some American companies that offer package tours there, but people taking these tours generally stay in four-star hotels. I didn't want to see Vietnam that way. Instead, I went to a search engine, Google, and typed in "Vietnam Tours." Instantly, I had a list of hundreds of Vietnamese companies that offered tours of every conceivable nature. I then spent about a week reasearching the various tours available.

I finally decided to take a "set departure" group tour with a Vietnamese company, TF Handspan Adventure Tours. It offered a twenty-one-day tour that started in Hanoi, went to most of the important sites, avoided tourist sites I didn't want to visit, and ended in Saigon/Ho Chi Minh City. Handspan books hard sleepers for the ten-hour train trip from Hanoi to Sapa, promising thin mattresses to make the trip more comfortable. For some reason, many people believe a direct relationship between being uncomfortable and authenticity; I didn't want to push that theory too far. There is another train to Sapa run by the Victoria hotel in Sapa, but it is quite expensive, so I decided to try my luck with the hard-sleeper trip and Handspan's mattresses.

I sent a message to the Handspan Web site and was quickly answered by someone who sent me additional information on the tour. I wanted to know how many people would be on the tour (six to eight people, usually, I was informed), and which hotels we'd be staying at. We had a choice of regular or superior hotels, and I chose regular ones because I wanted to avoid being isolated in fancy hotels, hoping to find more authenticity, but adequate comfort, in two-star ones. I looked up the hotels we'd be staying at in the guidebooks; they were all favorably reviewed.

The hotel Handspan uses for people on the tour, The Salute, would cost us $25.00 a night. For this amount of money, you can get a very nice hotel in Vietnam. However, by Vietnamese standards, it is not cheap; the price represents about one month's wages for a typical Vietnamese worker.

When I booked the tour on the Internet, the Handspan Web site said the tour would start on Saturday. I decided my wife and I would arrive a day early and then spend a couple of extra days in Saigon at the end of our tour. After I had bought my airline tickets, an employee of Handspan named Annie informed me that the tour would start on Monday. Fortunately, everything worked out; it meant I'd have more time in Hanoi before the tour began, to recuperate from the flight, and would leave on schedule from Saigon. It was lucky that I had given myself a few extra days.

Ironically, it soon appeared my wife and I would be the only people on the tour. I had spent a good deal of time looking for a "set departure" group tour that would presumably include other people with whom we could talk and interact. But being alone could have certain advantages for my purposes. For example, I might be able to get more information about Vietnamese culture and society from our guides. It certainly would be different from other group tours we'd taken in China and in Morocco, both of which had around fifteen people.

Over the course of six or eight weeks I must have exchanged twenty or thirty messages with Annie. I noticed a certain forwardness in Annie's correspondence. Sometimes she would send me a message asking what I did over the weekend. I assumed she was as curious about us as we were about her. Sometimes, she sent rather terse e-mail messages, probably because she had so much work to do. I have read many descriptions of Vietnamese women, with their hair down to their waists, wearing long white gloves, riding their motorbikes, and in some cases motorcycles, in Hanoi and Saigon. I wondered if she would be like that. Once she sent an e-mail message that contained a photograph of herself and a Vietnamese calendar as attachments.

Our tour, incidentally, would cost approximately $1,500 for the two of us. That included all our hotels, some meals, flights from Hanoi to Hue and from Da Nang to Saigon (approximately $300 for the two of us), many different boat trips, and admission to most museums and other sites. Handspan would be saving some money on us because we would be sleeping on the train trips from Hanoi to Sapa and back and staying on a boat while we cruised around Haiphong Bay. I tried to figure out how the company could make a profit at that price, but I assume they must.

I also had the problem of finding an airline to take us to Vietnam. Because we were starting our tour in Hanoi and ending it in Saigon, we needed an open-jaw ticket in order to fly into one city but return from another, and that turned out to be a real complication. One day I searched the Internet for "Vietnam Flights" and a travel agency in San Jose, California, Sunlight Travel, popped up. It had charts displaying the different airlines, their schedules for Vietnam, and prices. This travel agency is run by people of Vietnamese descent. I was able to arrange an open-jaw round-trip flight on Cathay Pacific at a relatively reasonable cost: $1,040 per person. If we were arriving at and departing from Saigon, the flight would have been a couple of hundred dollars cheaper. However, we needed to fly to Hanoi and return from Saigon/Ho Chi Minh City. It is not cheap to get to Vietnam, but once you are there, it is relatively inexpensive to travel, according to the guidebooks. The food is not expensive and our hotels were all covered (except for the first three days). Most of our breakfasts were included as well.

We each had to get a typhus shot, antirabies vaccines (three shots), some antimalaria medicine, and some other antiviral medicine, but that was easily taken care of by calling the travel nurse at the medical facility we use and scheduling appointments. I also purchased our travel insurance via the Internet, through a company we often use.

Finally, we needed to obtain our visas. One company I had contacted was kind enough to send us visa forms for Vietnam, so we duplicated them, filled them out, and attached the requisite photos. I couldn't find information on the Web regarding how much the fee for each visa was. Fortunately, I was able to obtain the phone number of the Vietnamese consulate in San Francisco. I called and found that visas cost $65.00 per person. So I got a cashier's check and sent our visa applications. A little more than a week later, the visas came. Everything was set for our visit to Vietnam.

Taking a trip like this, especially if you do it on your own, involves a certain amount of snooping around on the Internet and a considerable amount of e-mail message writing. All of this was, I thought, an introduction to Vietnamese culture. Finally, all that remained was actually taking the trip. And what would I find? I had heard of the fields with thirty shades of green, the areas of Hanoi that make you think you're in France. On the other hand, I had also heard of the frenzied motorized Vietnamese, buzzing around like race car drivers, and legions of beggars and pesty children.

Also, I must confess to a certain amount of anxiety about getting diarrhea in Vietnam. Many people do, so the guidebooks say, but generally it is very mild and one gets over it quickly. Still, having suffered from that affliction a number of different times during our vacations, I can't escape a sense of anxiety. It seems that writer Andrew Pham, when he visited Vietnam, had gastrointestinal troubles all the time. Would I also succumb? When we traveled in Morocco I was fine; an element of luck exists in travel and I hoped I'd be lucky this time. Just in case, I took precautions, from over the-counter remedies to prescription drugs. I happen to love Vietnamese food. We have a Vietnamese restaurant where I live whose claim to fame is that it was visited by Julia Child. It is little more than a hole-in-the-wall, but the food is extremely tasty. Every time I go there it seems I end up having conversations with people at adjoining tables, who are with *Wired* magazine or some new high-tech company.

So I found myself full of anticipation, with touches of anxiety, about our trip to Vietnam. A friend who had been there said "it's beyond being fabulous." My wife Phyllis and I wanted to find out for ourselves. Our itinerary gave an idea of what we'd be seeing in Vietnam:

TF HANDSPAN GROUP TOUR ITINERARY

Friday, June 29	Land in Hanoi. Until July 1 on our own, Salute Hotel.
Monday, July 2	Tour starts in Hanoi.
Tuesday, July 3	Tour of Hanoi and outskirts.
Wednesday, July 4	Haiphong Bay (sleep on boat).
Thursday, July 5	Cat Ba Island.
Friday, July 6	Cat Ba Island to Hanoi.

Saturday, July 7	Free day in Hanoi. Night train to Sapa (sleep on train).
Sunday, July 8	Sapa.
Monday, July 9	Sapa.
Tuesday, July 10	Sapa to Hanoi. Night train to Hanoi (sleep on train).
Wednesday, July 11	Free day in Hanoi.
Thursday, July 12	Hanoi-to-Hue flight.
Friday, July 13	Boat ride, bus to Hoi An.
Saturday, July 14	Hoi An.
Sunday, July 15	Hoi An.
Monday, July 16	Da Nang, flight to Ho Chi Minh City (Saigon).
Tuesday, July 17	Tour of Ho Chi Minh City/Saigon.
Wednesday, July 18	Tay Ninh: Cao Dai Cathedral and Cu Chi Tunnels.
Thursday, July 19	Cao Lanh boat trip. Stay in Chau Doc.
Friday, July 20	Boat trip. Can Tho.
Saturday, July 21	Can Tho boat trip. Return to Ho Chi Minh City/Saigon.
Sunday, July 22	Return flight to United States: 10:15 a.m. flight to Hong Kong; 11:20 p.m. Hong Kong to San Francisco, Cathay Pacific.

An outline like this gives one a sense of the scope of a trip; what it doesn't reveal are the people, the experiences, the scenery, the meals, and the sites in each city. It remains for me to fill in the details of this outline and to use my trip as a means of discovering, and sharing, interesting aspects of Vietnamese culture and everyday life. I was on a search for "signs" that reveal interesting facts about Vietnamese culture, and was curious about what I would find. From examining other tours on the Internet and reading various guidebooks I knew that, at the very least, I would be going to many of the most important sites in Vietnam.

ANNIE, THU, AND PROBLEMS WITH NAMES

When I first contacted my travel agency in Vietnam, I received an e-mail message from a young woman who, I believed, took care of the company's e-mail messages. Her name was Annie. Over the weeks, I sent her various questions and a few pieces I had written.

She answered my questions and added a good deal about herself. From the following letters I gained a sense of her personality.

> Dear Arthur,
>
> Thank you very much indeed for being so kind and sweet to me. My heart felt much warmer after receiving your email. Oh . . . you know . . . your concerns always do lift up my spirit. Once again, thanks for everything. It's coincidence! Today May 10th is my 25th birthday! . . . You'll find no better place for pho than in Hanoi. Do you want me to show? I can be your guide if . . . you request . . . he he he. . . . How does it sound to you? Await your message.
>
> Annie

I must have sent twenty or thirty e-mail messages to Annie over the course of the months before we left for Vietnam.

In another e-mail message she wrote:

> We haven't known each other long but we've shared each other's dreams. I've decided that together we make quite a perfect team. Though we're very different, we were brought together by a common bond. . . . Arthur, could you do me a favor??? A friend of mine who is living in San Francisco wants to send me an Internet modem 56K. I'm currently using the size 14K, which is very slow. If it's possible, could you please bring it over here for me?

I refused to do so, because I didn't want to get involved with customs in Vietnam, and most certainly with trying to sneak in a modem.

I found this message quite amusing. Annie passed me on to another colleague, Thu, who sent me information about my hotels. I wanted to find out whether a person I'd been corresponding with at the U.S. Embassy in Hanoi was a male or a female, so I asked Thu. That person's name was Ngo Dinh Quynh. I asked Thu whether "Ngo Dinh" was a male or a female's name, and she replied she'd never seen a name like that and that I must have left out part of the name. I had been corresponding with Quynh assuming that Quynh was a last name, but it turns out that it probably was a first name, and that Ngo was his or her last name. (I found out later that Ngo was his first name and Quynh was his last name. I was confused because I didn't know that in Vietnam people give their family names first.)

I had been sending e-mail messages to Quynh to set up several lectures that I had arranged to give in Hanoi. Because my wife and I were going there three days early, I had some free time and arranged to give two lectures and readings there.

When I used only my first name at the end of an e-mail, Quynh replied that in Vietnam that wasn't the practice, and that I could call Quynh by that name but that I should sign my messages with my full name. Quynh is an assistant in the cultural affairs office at the U.S. Embassy in Vietnam. I didn't hear from Quynh for a number of weeks and discovered that was because a hacker had disrupted the State Department's computers. Fortunately, Quynh had an alternative e-mail address and I was able to make contact using that address.

ADVENTURE WEAR AND MAGIC GLASSES: I GO HIGH TECH

I checked the weather for Vietnam in my guidebooks, and on the Internet, and all my sources indicated that it would be very hot and humid there. The average temperature is around ninety degrees with nearly 100 percent humidity. I decided to take precautions to avoid getting sunburned and being any more uncomfortable than was necessary. And so began a long search through various Internet sites of companies that sold travel clothes, places like REI, L.L.Bean, and RailRiders, as I looked for shirts and pants that would shield me from the sun and keep me as comfortable as possible.

A dermatologist I consulted had suggested I buy clothing made of Supplex nylon to protect myself from the sun. I purchased a wide-brimmed hat, a long-sleeved shirt, and a pair of pants made of this nylon. It is one of the new "wonder" fabrics that is very light, very tough, dries in a few hours when washed, and protects you from the sun.

After looking at various sites and being shocked by the prices these garments cost, I happened on RailRiders, which has an overstock section, and purchased an Aero shirt for $29, marked down from $70, and a pair of Weatherpants, for $49, marked down from $75. These Weatherpants were described on the Internet as follows:

Constructed from Supplex DuPont nylon, they are soft and supple to the touch, but amazingly abrasion-and-tear-resistant. Cordura seat and knee patches will keep python fangs and sharp-edged volcanic rocks at bay. And yet they weigh a scant 11 oz., and can be folded or rolled into a small, packable bundle, but will still shake out wrinkle-free. With a 15-minute drying time, the fast-evaporating fabric will keep your legs cool and sun-protected in tropical heat or warm in mid-afternoon downpours. . . . Whether you're an SUV-driving urban commando or born-in-the-backcountry, these Weatherpants make the perfect fashion statement for adventuring.

I felt I simply had to have these pants to go with my two-ply, three-ounce Akwadyne Supplex molecular fabric Aero shirt with torso vents, a back vent with mesh, low-profile zippered-front pockets, and a Coolmax mesh insert. The Internet advertisement for this shirt stated:

You won't need a science degree to appreciate the technological wonders of the fastest-drying shirt in the world. Constructed from electrostatic akwadyne supplex nylon, the fabric literally soaks up you [sic] sweat like a smart sponge and molecularly spreads it across the fibers for rapid evaporation. Perspiration is literally suctioned away from your skin.

I figured it was important to have these fantastic garments to shield me from the sun. They also dry in a few hours, making it possible to travel "light."

I also couldn't help but wonder whether these garments would work. It might be that plain cotton and other natural fabrics would actually be better and so I decided to bring a silk shirt, a thin cotton shirt, and some cotton pants along, just in case.

We test washed my Aero shirt and Weatherpants and they dried very quickly. That made me think that at least I wouldn't have to worry about my clothes drying overnight. In theory I could wash my shirt every night and wear it the next day. My wife read about the mosquitos in Vietnam in the tour books and I persuaded her to get a long-sleeved Supplex shirt from RailRiders. In addition, while cruising the Internet, looking at the various adventure-clothing sites, I came across the REI overstock section and found they had Terramar (another so-called miracle fabric) T-shirts on sale for only $6.97 each. I bought two, thinking it might be useful to have a quick-drying T-shirt in Vietnam.

A few new "miracle" fibers that adventure-clothing manufacturers use are Supplex, Terramar, CoolMax, Tactel, Tencel, and microfiber. These products help people avoid having cotton clothes getting heavy and uncomfortable when they are soaked by perspiration or water. Of course, cotton takes a good deal of time to dry, especially in climates with high humidity. I could only wonder: Will these new fabrics magically "whisk away" the perspiration, the way ads for them say they will, when we are in hot and muggy Vietnam?

It so happened that I was due to get new glasses; instead of getting a pair of sunglasses and another pair of regular glasses, I opted for a pair of so-called "transition" glasses that darken when exposed to sunlight and that provide excellent protection from the sun. So it would be a high-tech tourist who would land in Hanoi, with various miracle fibers and magical transition glasses!

The important question, actually, was what would I see, not what my glasses would be like. With my Supplex shirt and pants busy wicking away moisture and my transition glasses changing from light to dark, a lot would be going on, as far as my glasses and my clothes were concerned, even while I'd be standing still.

TEACHING THE VIETNAMESE
ABOUT AMERICAN CULTURE

In addition to touring Vietnam, as I mentioned earlier, I had arranged to give two readings and lectures in Hanoi about American culture and society. When we had finalized the plans for our visit, I got in touch with the U.S. Embassy there and informed them that I would be in Hanoi for a number of days and would be interested in meeting Vietnamese scholars and giving some lectures. I got an immediate response from an assistant cultural attaché there named Ngo Dinh Quynh asking me whether I expected to get paid for my lectures or would give the lectures for free, or for a nominal price. "We don't have much money," he said.

I said I'd be happy to lecture for free. He asked me for some topics I might lecture on, and I sent a list. We decided that I would give readings and lectures from my comic mystery *Postmortem for a Post-modernist* (1997) on postmodernism, and from my book on everyday life in the United States, *Bloom's Morning* (1997). I was told that some of the people in the group attending the postmodernism lecture wouldn't know English, so Quynh arranged for me to have an interpreter for that lecture. That meant I wouldn't be able to cover as much territory as I would have liked, but I'd do the best I could.

Quynh wanted me to give three lectures, but I decided that it was too much, so we settled on two. I was curious how they would be received. Would anyone even be at my lectures? Both of my books have a whimsical, comic aspect to them and I wondered if my audience would "get" my humor. It was quite possible; I'd had very good luck with the Chinese, who have translated both *Postmortem for a Post-modernist* and *Bloom's Morning,* and a number of my other books, into their language. I could only wonder how the Vietnamese would respond to them.

ESCAPING WITH ONE'S LIFE
WHILE TOURING VIETNAM

The guidebooks can scare the hell out of you with information on all the diseases and problems with pickpockets and other situations you might face in Vietnam. In a chapter titled "Dangers & Annoyances: Culture Shock," Florence and Storey, the authors of the *Lonely Planet Vietnam* (1999) write:

> Before reunification, street crime was rampant in the South, especially in Saigon. Motorbike-borne thieves (called cowboys by the Americans) would speed down major thoroughfares, ripping pedestrians' watches off their wrists. Pickpocketing and confidence tricks were also common. . . . We have had countless reports of street crime, particularly in Saigon, and regardless of how safe it may seem, you should always exercise caution and common sense. One strong suggestion for Saigon is do not have anything dangling off your body that you are not ready to part with. This includes bags, and any jewelry—even of the costume variety, which might tempt a robber.

Especially watch out for drive-by-thieves on motorbikes—they specialize in snatching handbags and cameras from tourists walking in the city and riding in cyclos. Some have become proficient at grabbing valuables from the open window of a car and speeding away with the loot. Foreigners have occasionally reported having their eyeglasses and hats snatched, too.

Pickpocketing—often involving kids, women with babies and newspaper vendors—is also a serious problem, especially in tourist areas of Saigon such as Dong Khoi and the Pham Ngu Lao area. Many of the street kids, adorable as they may be, are very skilled at liberating people from their wallets or whatever else might be in their pocket or handbag. (p. 119)

The authors then move on to discussions of violence, scams, beggar fatigue, undetonated explosives, sea creatures, and noise. In the forests you have to look out for poisonous snakes, too.

When I read this material, and the warnings in my other guidebook, *The Rough Guide to Vietnam* (Dodd and Lewis, 2000), I wondered, for a moment, whether I was visiting Vietnam to have a pleasant vacation or to challenge the fates, with little chance of surviving without undergoing some kind of trauma. Of course, travel always involves an element of risk, and you read the same kind of warnings about Thailand and many other countries, but this seemed to be quite extreme. Vietnam is a very poor country and many desperate people live in it. I would imagine the authors were exaggerating to alert readers to possible problems they may encounter, to help them avoid being victimized.

It's easy to understand why a tourist might become slightly paranoid about going to Vietnam, when they are told that every woman with a baby is a potential pickpocket or some other kind of criminal. As a result of reading these guides, and others as well, my wife and I decided to wear travel pouches underneath our clothes. But how we would deal with carrying more than one million dong around with us (a packet the size of a brick) remained to be seen. If, for example, you change one hundred dollars into 10,000-dong notes, you end up with around 140 of them—quite a load. Even if you were to get seventy 20,000-dong notes, you would still have a big wad of money to deal with. Of course we would divide that stash into half, so my wife and I would each only be carrying relatively small bricks of money.

A RAINBOW THE DAY WE LEAVE

Almost all the flights to Vietnam that I investigated left around 12:30 a.m., and our flight was no different. That means we had the whole day to relax, check over our travel bags (we each decided to take one small bag), and get ourselves set for the long trip. It rained in the morning, but around 7:00 p.m., I looked out the window of my study and a beautiful rainbow had touched down about 200 feet below our house. *That must mean something good,* I thought.

ON THE MATTER OF VIETNAM'S APPEAL
FOR TOURISTS

For those tourists visiting Vietnam, Saigon hasn't fallen off the map, and neither has Hanoi. Indeed, Vietnam is becoming an increasingly important tourism destination; more and more Americans and people from other nations are visiting the country. The questions that interested me most, as I sat down to consider tourism in Vietnam were: What does Vietnam have to offer tourists? What is the secret of its appeal? How do you explain the impact the country makes upon tourists who visit it? What objects do tourists encounter and what places do they go that are meaningful for them? Some scholars have suggested that tourism involves, in essence, consuming "signs." If that is the case, what signs typify Vietnam for tourists? These are the questions I deal with in the next part of this book, "Semiotic Vietnam."

PART III:
SEMIOTIC VIETNAM—
INTERPRETING THE COUNTRY

There is a series of phenomena of great importance which cannot possibly be recorded by questioning or computing documents, but have to be observed in their full actuality. Let us call them the imponderabilia of actual life. Here belong such things as the routine of a man's working day, the details of his care of the body, of the manner of taking food and preparing it; the tone of conversational and social life around the village fires, the existence of strong friendships or hostilities, and of passing sympathies and dislikes between people; the subtle yet unmistakable manner in which personal vanities and ambitions are reflected in the behaviour of the individual and in the emotional reactions of those who surround him. All these facts can and ought to be scientifically formulated and recorded, but it is necessary that this be done, not by a superficial registration of details, as is usually done by untrained observers, but with an effort at penetrating the mental attitude expressed in them.

Bronislaw Malinowski,
Argonauts of the Western Pacific

The objects which surround us do not simply have utilitarian aspects; rather they serve as a kind of mirror which reflects our own image. Objects which surround us permit us to discover more and more aspects of ourselves. . . . In a sense, therefore, a knowledge of the soul of things is possibly a direct and new and revolutionary way of discovering the soul of man.

Ernest Dichter,
The Strategy of Desire

Chapter 5

Understanding Vietnam: Culture and Geography

In an article about a recent trip to Italy to see the Leaning Tower of Pisa, travel writer John Flinn discusses the way tourists in the 1960s saw the world. He writes (2003, p. C3): "Every European country was reduced to a quick, cartoonish cliché: France was the Eiffel Tower, England was Big Ben, Spain a bullfighter, Holland a windmill and Italy, of course, the Leaning Tower." His experience of seeing the tower, however, caused him to rethink his "jaded attitude toward those clichéd icons. Maybe they're worth visiting after all," he added.

Generally speaking, when tourists return from visiting a foreign country, they bring back memories of various experiences they had in the form of mental images. Flinn describes them as "archetypal travel images that sleep in your subconscious." These images tend to be of people they've met, objects that attracted their attention, and places of great natural beauty or cultural interest they've seen. All of these are what semioticians call "signs."

After I discuss scholarly approaches to studying cultures and explain some fundamental aspects of semiotics, I will analyze and interpret a number of the most important Vietnamese signs, such as *pho,* spring rolls, conical straw hats, and *ao dai* costumes, signs that function as archetypal images of Vietnam for tourists.

SCHOLARLY APPROACHES TO STUDYING FOREIGN CULTURES

The quotations by Malinowski and Dichter that begin this section offer an important insight into ways of analyzing a culture. Tourists travel because, among other things, they want to gain insights into everyday life in whatever country they are visiting. The great anthropologist Malinowski talked about the "imponderabilia" of everyday life—the objects people use, the rituals they practice, the routines they observe for cooking and eating food, the tone of their social life—all of these things give tourists a sense of what the country they are visiting is really like. They offer insights into what we can describe as a country's collective psyche and national character.

Another writer who provides us with a methodology for understanding foreign cultures is the French semiotician Roland Barthes, one of the most influential thinkers of recent years. His book about the "myths" that pervade everyday life in France, *Mythologies* (1972), is considered a classic, and so is his book about distinctive aspects of everyday life in Japan, *Empire of Signs* (1982). In the following section, I will briefly describe semiotics and the method of analysis that Barthes uses, and then I will offer an example of his style of writing, namely his discussion of sukiyaki and Japanese cuisine.

THE IDEAS OF ROLAND BARTHES

The Semiotics of Cultures

Let me begin this discussion of semiotics with Barthes' *Empire of Signs,* his elegant and incisive study of Japanese culture. Barthes' style, I should point out, is quite distinctive: at times it is quite poetic and lyrical and at other times it is very complicated and somewhat opaque. In this book he writes about his fascination with Japan:

> If I want to imagine a fictive nation, I can give it an invented name, treat it declaratively as a novelistic object, create a new Garabagne, so as to compromise no real country by my fantasy (though it is then that fantasy itself I compromise by the signs of literature). I can also—though in no way claiming to represent or to analyze reality (these being the major gestures of Western discourse)—isolate somewhere in the world *(faraway)* a certain number of features (a term employed in linguistics), and out of these features deliberately form a system. It is this system which I shall call: Japan. (p. 3)

What Barthes does in *Empire of Signs* is to analyze certain Japanese objects, places, and practices that struck him as significant. The book has twenty-seven short chapters, generally three to four pages in length, on such topics as Japanese chopsticks, sukiyaki, tempura, *pachinko* (a gambling game), packages, train stations, stationery stores, and spatial organization. Each chapter reveals interesting and important facts about Japan.

Semiotics, the methodology Barthes employs, is defined as the science of the signs. (The Greek term *sēmeîon* means sign.) One of the founding fathers of semiotics, the Swiss linguist Ferdinand de Saussure, explained that signs are composed of two elements—sound-images *(signifiers)* and concepts *(signifieds)*. A sound-image, such as a word, stands for a concept or idea, but it is important to recognize that the relationship that exists between a sound-image and a concept is arbitrary and based on convention. That is, one has to learn what signs mean.

de Saussure explains the structure of signs as follows:

> I propose to retain the word sign (signe) to designate the whole and to replace *concept* and *sound-image* respectively by *signified (signifié)* and *signifier (significant)*; the last two terms have the advantage of indicating the opposition that separates them from each other and from the whole of which they are parts. (1966, p. 67)

Signs are, then, like pieces of paper: one side is the signifier and the other side is the signified. Signs, in the most general sense, are anything that can stand for something else. Thus, for example, body language, facial expressions, clothing, and body ornaments are signs, revealing aspects of a person (if we know how to interpret these signs, that is). The science of semiotics is extremely complicated, and we need not go into it any further. What we must do is recognize that a semiotic analysis of a culture involves looking for important signs and interpreting them to discern what they reveal about the culture.

Rawness in Japanese Food

Let me offer a brief example of semiotic analysis from Barthes' *Empire of Signs*. In this selection he discusses "rawness," an important signifier of Japanese food. This analysis is found in his chapter "Food Decentered" which begins with a discussion of sukiyaki:

Sukiyaki is a stew whose every element can be known and recognized, since it is made in front of you, on your table, without
interruption while you are eating it. The raw substances (but
peeled, washed, already garbed in an aesthetic nakedness, shiny,
bright-colored, harmonious as a spring garment: *"color, delicacy, touch, effect, harmony, relish—everything can be found
here . . ."* (1982, p. 19)

Barthes moves on, shortly after this passage, to speculations about
the meaning of rawness. He writes:

This Rawness, we know, is the tutelary divinity of Japanese
food: to it everything is dedicated, and if Japanese cooking is always performed in front of the eventual diner (a fundamental
feature of this cuisine), this is probably because it is important to
consecrate by spectacle the death of what is being honored. . . .
Japanese rawness is essentially visual; it denotes a certain col-
ored state of the flesh or vegetable substance (it being understood that color is never exhausted by a catalogue of tints, but
refers to a whole tactility of substance; thus *sashimi* exhibits not
so much colors as resistances: those which vary the flesh of raw
fish, causing it to pass from one end of the tray to the other,
through the stations of the soggy, the fibrous, the elastic, the
compact, the rough, the slippery). Entirely visual (conceived,
concerted, manipulated for sight, and even for a painter's eye),
food thereby says that it is not *deep:* the edible substance is
without a precious heart, without a buried power, without a visual secret: no Japanese dish is endowed with a *center . . .* here
everything is the ornament of another ornament. (1982, p. 20)

What Barthes does, then, in his inimitable style, is take Japanese
signs that he believes have important cultural resonance and explain
their deeper meaning and cultural significance. Japan, he writes, is an
"empire of signifiers" (1982, p. 9) of enormous interest; in his book
Barthes takes upon himself the task of explaining what these signifiers reveal.

Donald Richie, an expert on Japanese culture, has stated that Japanese have their own special ways of doing everything. Richie offered
some insights into Japanese culture in a 1962 interview. He noted that
when one thinks about Japan, one should think about the importance

of form in everyday life, and the social patterns that exist there: "There is a way to pay calls, a way to go shopping, a way to drink tea, a way to arrange flowers, a way to owe money. A formal absolute exists and is aspired to" (quoted in French, 2001, p. B6).

Richie believes that these forms are necessary to prevent social chaos. Other countries, he points out, also have rituals of various kinds to help order life, but in Japan these forms and rituals end up as what might be described as an art of behavior. Vietnam isn't the same as Japan, which has what might be called a much more formalized culture. An order to life in Vietnam is to be discovered and beliefs, attitudes, and values are to be discerned there.

Vietnam, from what I've learned, isn't as "formal," in Richie's use of the term, as Japan and is much more eclectic and combinatory. Vietnam's culture represents, it seems, a *fusion,* a blending of things from many different cultures—Chinese, Indian, Thai, French, and American—that greatly influenced it. This fusion has a very unique nature to it, and I believe there exists something distinctive in Vietnamese culture. That is what I was interested in exploring.

It was important to me to find signs and symbols—objects, practices, heroes, places, foods, phenomena, or, to cite Malinowski's term, "imponderabilia," that offer insights into Vietnamese character and culture, in the same way that signs such as people's facial expressions, body language, voice, dress, and hairstyles offer insights into their personalities and character.

My travels through Vietnam enabled me to find a number of interesting signs that I have interpreted to offer insights into the nature of Vietnamese culture and society. I won't be trying to read the universe in a grain of sand, but I will be trying to read Vietnamese culture in a conical straw hat or a bowl of *pho.*

QUOC NGU:
THE VIETNAMESE WRITTEN LANGUAGE

When you go to Vietnam, you notice that all the signs are written in a Romanized script instead of Chinese characters *(chu nho)*. The Vietnamese wrote with Chinese characters until the fourteenth century, when they developed their own script, called *chu nom*. This was supplanted by *Quoc Ngu,* a romanized script developed in the seven-

Shop fronts show what the Vietnamese language looks like. Foreigners can read the words, since they are written in a roman script, but generally don't have any notion of what the words mean.

teenth century by a French priest, Alexandre de Rhodes. In Vietnamese, since every syllable is considered to be an independent word, the language appears to be monosyllabic, though some linguists argue that it really is polysyllabic.

Vietnamese is tonal in nature, having six tones: low rising, high rising, low broken, high broken, mid-level, and low falling. These tones are indicated by five diacritical marks and an unmarked tone. Thus, people from Western countries may be able to "read" Vietnamese when they see it on store signs, street signs, and menus, but they won't understand very much, even if they think they know what the word means.

Depending upon the markings, as Dodd and Lewis (2000) point out, "the word *ba* can mean three, grandmother, poisoned food, waste, aunt or any—leaving ample scope for misunderstandings and diplomatic incidents" (p. 488). Thus the Vietnamese language is more difficult to understand than many other languages that use a Romanized alphabet, but don't have the tones and are based on Latin, such as French and Spanish.

This problem of interpreting Vietnamese words may be a metaphor for the difficulty I faced trying to make sense of Vietnamese culture and, in general, any analysis of Vietnamese culture by a foreigner. I can read some words in Vietnamese signs but because I don't know what the diacritical marks indicate, I can't be sure that I know what anything really means. It doesn't take long to learn certain words—for example, *kem* is ice cream and *com* is rice. But you don't learn a lot of Vietnamese on your own.

When I was in Hanoi, I had lunch with someone from the U.S. Embassy. He told me he could speak and read Russian and Japanese, but that Vietnamese was too difficult for him to master. He could understand a good deal of what he read in newspapers but couldn't express himself well using the language. This was after six months of studying Vietnamese for five hours a day. Another interesting fact about the language is that because Vietnamese has so many single-syllable words, when people speak it, it has a kind of singsong effect.

It may be that when I observed Vietnamese daily life, I could see what was going on but I didn't understand the complexities in what I saw as much as I thought I did. That is, our ability to "read" *Quoc Ngu* but not understand what it means may be a telling metaphor for the problems foreigners face when trying to understand Vietnamese culture. This culture is an enigma for tourists that often seems, on the face of things, deceptively simple; but it is actually very complex and highly nuanced, like its language.

THE CAO DAI CATHEDRAL AT TAY NINH

Cao Dai means "high tower" or "high palace," which is, for the followers of the Cao Dai religion, another way of saying God. The Cao Dai Cathedral is one of those architectural curiosities that one can only imagine in one's dreams. When you look at it from the outside, you realize it is a truly fantastic building; it is bizarre beyond comparison. When you go inside, it is even wilder; you see many ornate pink columns full of dragons and snakes and other extraordinary things. The cathedral takes on a kind of hyperkitsch quality that somehow transcends kitsch and makes you wonder whether you've wandered into some crazed architect's dream or nightmare.

The cathedral is, beyond doubt, the wildest, zaniest building I've ever seen, in part because of the use of gaudy colors (which the Vietnamese probably picked up from the Chinese) and in part because of the hypereclectic hodgepodge of decorations and symbols, including a gigantic globe with a huge eye, with which the cathedral is decorated. The cathedral reflects the eclecticism of the religion itself, which tries to blend elements of Buddhism, Confucianism, Taoism, Islam, and Christianity, as revealed through certain "saints" such as William Shakespeare, Winston Churchill, Joan of Arc, Victor Hugo, and Napoleon Bonaparte. Revelations from these saints were, it seems, discovered by a spiritualist who used a planchette, a pencil secured to a wooden board on casters on which a medium rests his hands and writes what the saints communicate to him. Adherents of Cao Dai also use séances to obtain divine guidance.

The religion was created in 1926 by a spiritualist named Ngo Van Chieu, who worked as a civil servant and was contacted, he says, by a "supreme being" called Cao Dai, who instructed him on Cao Dai's tenets and told him to use the divine eye as its symbol. The Cao Dai priests, who are all laypersons, are asked to pray four times a day: at midnight, six o'clock in the morning, noon, and six o'clock in the evening. The adherents believe that Cao Dai is a transcendent religion and that it has attained a level beyond all other religions. These other religions are seen as valid but not as elevated or synoptic as Cao Dai.

The Cao Dai religion also has a pope, an idea they picked up from Roman Catholicism.

While in Vietnam, I watched part of the noon service. A group of about 100 people, in various costumes, some in red robes, some in yellow robes, some in blue robes, and most in white robes, filed into the Cao Dai Cathedral and sat down, clasping their hands together. In the balcony, a small band and a chorus of musicians played music and chanted prayers. I wasn't there long enough to see what else happened, but the part that I saw was quite curious. No one spoke, though the adherents may have been praying silently. They just sat, while the band played and the chorus sang.

Cao Daism is, I believe, a signifier of an important element of Vietnamese character and culture: the ability to incorporate elements from outside Vietnam into its culture and come up with something that is distinctive and unique. This ability to create fusions between disparate and sometimes contrasting or conflicting elements may be part of the genius of contemporary Vietnamese culture.

An estimated 2 million people believe in Cao Dai. One finds hundreds of smaller Cao Dai temples scattered throughout the southern part of Vietnam, and as far north as Hue. Graham Greene, it is alleged, once seriously considered converting from Catholicism to Cao Daism. (He concluded, after investigating it, that it was full of nonsense.)

This cathedral is one of the most important tourism sites in Vietnam and is on most tourist itineraries. It is a kind of curiosity that intrigues tourists and intensifies the sense that many tourists have that Vietnam is, in many ways, a remarkable place to visit. Vietnam has something that tourists crave—a vibrant and extremely fascinating culture.

SAPA AND THE HILL-TRIBE GIRLS

One can get to Sapa, a beautiful hill city in the northwest of Vietnam, in a number of ways. You can go by bus or car, take a very slow overnight train whose best accommodations are "hard sleepers" (six people in a compartment on hard wooden beds), or take a "soft sleeper" run by Victoria Hotels and stay at the Victoria Hotel in Sapa, the best hotel in the city—and the most expensive, by far. The trains don't take you to Sapa but to Lo Cai, where you can get buses or taxis to take you up the winding roads to Sapa. The train takes ten hours and the drive to Sapa from Lo Cai takes an hour and half. As you ride up through the hills toward Sapa, you can look out on truly spectacular scenery—incredible terraces where rice is grown that snake up very high hills. It must have taken prodigious amounts of work to make those terraces and it must take enormous effort to maintain them. In Sapa, you will find gorgeous vistas of the surrounding areas.

Sapa is a city full of hotels, restaurants, and stores that cater to tourists. Some sections of Sapa are residential, but the downtown area of Sapa is devoted to tourism. Main attractions in Sapa include the people from the hill tribes that live in settlements near the city—the Black Hmong and Red Zhao. Other hill-tribe settlements exist farther away from the city.

In Sapa, the young girls from the hill tribes interact most with the tourists, though you also find many middle-aged and older hill-tribe women there. They are all selling handicrafts. When you eat in a restaurant, its not unusual for three or four women to stand outside and show you their crafts. They are not allowed inside the restaurants. They can be a bit of a nuisance, but their efforts seem innocent, and if you shake your head, they generally retreat.

On Friday and Saturday evenings, men and women of the hill tribes hold concerts playing various instruments, dancing, and singing. These concerts take place in the bar of the Green Bamboo Hotel (generally considered the second-best hotel in town), where tourists and throngs of young Black Hmong and Red Zhao girls congregate, selling bracelets and mouth harps and other items. Their mothers also are there, keeping track of things. You might see them urging their daughters on.

These little girls, most of them between the ages of eight and ten, are incredibly charming and delightful, though they are also always trying to sell things. They all speak English and some speak other languages such as French, German, and Italian, which they learn from the tourists who visit the city. The phrase they've learned best and use most is "Will you buy from me?"

Sometimes you see the men from the Black Hmong trudging through town with grim looks on their faces. You don't see Black Hmong men very often—they stay in the background and let their little sisters do the charming and the selling. The Black Hmong and Red

Zhao add a great deal of color, both literally and figuratively, to Sapa, and are a tourist attraction of considerable significance. In the United States, not many people (aside from Native Americans and members of some religious sects) wear traditional costumes that haven't changed for hundreds of years and live in such simple and primitive conditions.

There's something exotic and fascinating, and yet disturbing, about seeing these hill-tribe people. They are holding on to their traditional ways of living while watching, on the television sets at the Green Bamboo Bar, two nights a week, a world that is much different from the one they inhabit, one that is probably as strange to them as theirs is to many of us.

THE MEKONG DELTA

There's something rather wonderful about the Mekong Delta, but it's difficult to put it into words. When I was a tourist there, I spent a good deal of time in boats of different sizes, sailing along rivers and through canals and in tiny streams. Everywhere you look, so it seems, the water spreading out before you is brown. Children play in it; women rinse vegetables and clean dishes in it; and much of the traveling and commerce in the Mekong region is done on it.

In the early evening, you often see people shampooing their hair in the water. As you glide through the waterways, little children wave their hands, smile, and shout "Hello!" Along the waterways you can see small houses, some well built and others made of little more than wood and palm leaves thatched together. Life in the Mekong Delta seems incredibly simple and elemental, if not primitive, especially along the rivers and canals.

The Mekong Delta is the third-largest delta in the world. The farmers there grow a large percentage of the food grown in Vietnam and, unlike other parts of the country, can have as many as three rice harvests. In the delta, people have fish farms in pens built underneath large boats. One will find wonderful floating markets. The famers attach samples of the fruits and vegetables they are selling to the fronts of their boats.

Boats by the thousands, generally run-down, of every size and kind, frequent the delta. The Vietnamese row the smaller ones by standing up on a small platform and pushing the oars in front of them in a scissors stroke. Some drive larger motor-driven boats that have strange-looking outboard motors with very long driveshafts. It is not unusual to see a young boy relaxing while steering his boat with a bare foot on the rudder.

The vegetation is tropical; tall palm trees are everywhere and give the landscape a kind of lotusland quality. Numerous places along the banks of the river are good, small areas to catch fish with nets. During the American War, in one hidden outpost in the Mekong Delta, the Vietcong established military headquarters. To get to this site, you take a small boat that can only hold four people. The boat barely makes it through incredibly thick vegetation that clusters on both sides of a tiny and very shallow stream. After twenty minutes, you end up in a clearing, with some small buildings, in which Vietcong officers planned their attacks.

But that was thirty years ago. It seems lost in history, just as contemporary society and its problems seem terribly distant when you are in the Mekong Delta. Before you, wherever you look, is the brown water. You see the ubiquitous palm trees, the clumps of water hyacinth penned up along the banks of the rivers, the houses, the children; it's like being in a different world, a world that, before you saw the Mekong Delta, you could only imagine, could only dream about.

Automobiles and, of course, motorbikes are ever-present on the small side roads in the delta. But life there seems to reduce itself to the bare essentials. You find yourself in this beautiful delta, cutting you off, if only for a brief interlude, from the turbulent world just one hundred miles away in Ho Chi Minh City.

A number of good-sized cities and towns are located in the Mekong Delta, and as you drive along the highways, or ride along them in buses, you see cafés with plastic chairs arranged neatly around tables or with lawn chairs, all arranged facing the highway. You see many houses, all with their doors and windows open. People in the Mekong Delta have a reputation for being very friendly. "They don't lock their doors, and if you get into a conversation with people in the Mekong, they most likely will invite you to their homes for dinner," someone had told me.

My wife and I spent three lovely days there, even though our trip involved spending countless hours on a bus and some "perilous" adventures getting in and out of many different boats. I left the Mekong

Delta with the feeling that I'd like to return, that there was something remarkable about the place, though I can't explain why I feel that way. My wife and I were with a group of about twenty tourists on that trip and they all had similar feelings about the Mekong's magic. Perhaps it was an ineffable feeling of peacefulness and joy, maybe even bliss (a word much beloved by Roland Barthes), that I felt as I traveled along its seemingly endless waterways.

HANOI

Shortly after I returned from Vietnam, a front-page article, "Good Morning Hanoi," by reporter David Armstrong appeared in the travel section of the Sunday *San Francisco Chronicle* (August 5, 2001). He explains that Hanoi, the capital of Vietnam, has a reputation as a stuffy, conservative, and even somewhat officious city, unlike Ho Chi Minh City (Saigon) in the south, which gets all the "buzz" and which is where all the "action" is supposed to take place. This image of Hanoi, he suggests, is mistaken: "I was expecting something Stalinist, something drab, and more than a little residual anger toward Americans, the legacy of what Vietnamese call 'the American War.' But, save for a few slabs of imposing seat-of-government architecture, Hanoi is anything but drab" (p. T1).

Because Ha Noi (or Hanoi, as Americans call it) is the capital of Vietnam, and because Vietnam is a communist state, many people have a foolish stereotype and expect it to be repressive and dull, an Asian version of Stalinist Moscow. That's not the case at all. Although Vietnam is officially a communist state, with communists running the government, in actuality Hanoi is full of budding capitalists, and some rather large-scale capitalists, as well.

Hanoi has many lakes and a number of areas with buildings built by the French during the colonial period, so it has a somewhat French or Mediterranean spirit, strange as it might seem. Literally speaking, Ha Noi means "City within the river's bend," which suggests the importance of the river to the city and the constraints that the river places on Hanoi.

One part of central Hanoi might seem like a thousand-year-old shopping mall, with certain streets devoted to specific products. One street is devoted to shoes, another to tin- and metal-work, another to

In Hanoi, visitors will find constant traffic—but not necessarily cars. Most of the traffic is in the form of mopeds and motorbikes. It is said that to cross the street in Hanoi, you must "close your eyes and keep walking."

straw goods, and another to tombstones. This part of the old city is, then, a prototype of the modern shopping mall, except that Hanoi's "shopping mall" has character and charm and is not plastic and sterile, like most contemporary shopping malls in the United States and elsewhere.

Hanoi, like many Asian cities, suffers from what I call "hyper-motorbike-ization." The streets of the old city, and many other parts of Hanoi, are clogged with people on motorbikes, the most popular means of motorized transportation in the city. The motorbike is to Vietnam what the automobile is to America.

One thing I like about Hanoi is that the downtown area is relatively small and you can walk to most of the sites you might want to see. As you walk on the streets of Hanoi, you see an endless succession of small restaurants, Internet cafés, *bia hoi* (cheap beer) joints, hotels, tourist agencies, clothing stores, electronics stores, local markets, and various other kinds of stores. And the sidewalks are full of parked motorbikes and street vendors, which means it is difficult, and in certain places almost impossible, to walk on the sidewalks in Hanoi. That's because life is lived on the sidewalks and streets of Hanoi and in the areas around the lakes.

Hoan Kiem Lake is the most important one in the city; people are always walking around it, sitting on benches and talking with friends, selling postcards and other items. In the early morning, many people go to the lake to do tai chi and play badminton, among other activities. Hoan Kiem Lake is a precious reserve of tranquillity; in contrast, the motorbikes whirl by around it endlessly, each driver honking his or her horn almost without stop.

If Hanoi is a big surprise, so is the rest of Vietnam. You don't get any sense that people are bitter about the American War or hate Americans, even though they have a war museum in Ho Chi Minh City with terrible photographs from the war. On the contrary, the Vietnamese are very friendly and go out of their way to be helpful to tourists. Hanoi also is a city full of wonderful restaurants, such as the Bittet restaurant, which is about ten minutes from Hoan Kiem Lake.

To get to the Bittet, you walk down a narrow passageway and through a small kitchen where four or five chefs are cooking away furiously. The restaurant is a large room with a number of long tables. For around $1.50 you can get a salad, a crispy baguette, an excellent little steak with a delicious sauce, superb French-fried potatoes, and something to drink. Some tourists, terrified by their guidebooks, don't eat the salads.

HO CHI MINH CITY/SAIGON

Ho Chi Minh City has an identity problem. Officially, it is known as Ho Chi Minh City but it is popularly known as Saigon, which is what it was called until the communists took over and renamed it in 1975. It got its original name due to its location on the bank of the Saigon River. Many people, especially people from the southern areas of Vietnam, still call it that.

The fact that the city has two names is interesting. The postwar Saigon identity is one which American troops helped fashion, where people are chasing the almighty dollar and the not-so-mighty dong. As a guide said to me when we arrived in Saigon, "People here make three times as much as people in other parts of Vietnam . . . and it's easy to spend it here, too."

If you were to think about these two cities in terms of the two dominant cities in California, Hanoi is San Francisco, and Ho Chi Minh City/Saigon is Los Angeles, with, perhaps, a touch of Las Vegas thrown in. Ho Chi Minh City is really a city-state or province, covering a huge area (2,030 square kilometers, which is approximately 50 kilometers by 40 kilometers or 30 miles by 24 miles) with an estimated 6, and perhaps as many as 8 million people, many of whom are from the countryside who have come to seek their fortunes in the big city. Tourists mostly visit the downtown (District 1) area and the Chinese region (Cholon).

Ho Chi Minh City is the name the communist bureaucrats in Hanoi would like to give the city, but it is too late to change the look of Saigon. Like Hanoi, it has a decidedly French influence, and its ethos is almost Western. It is a bustling and energetic place where there's a great deal of construction going on all the time and where, during rush hour, as in Hanoi, an awesome number of motorbikes, automobiles, cyclos, trucks, and buses fill the streets.

There's not a great deal to see in Saigon from a touristic point of view; in one or two days you can see most of the sites of interest. Most tourists go to the war museum, the reunification palace, the cathedral, the Chinese market in Cholon (District 5) and perhaps to some temples or pagodas. However, Saigon is close enough to the Cu

Chi Tunnels and Cao Dai Cathedral to make it possible to see them both in one day trip. It also is close to the Mekong Delta, which takes a few days to see.

Let me explain the differences between the city's old name (Saigon) and new name (Ho Chi Minh City) and how these names affect the city's image:

Saigon	Ho Chi Minh City
Old name	New identity
Popular identity	Official identity
What southerners call it	What northerners call it
French/American influence	Communist/socialist influence
Money: Make dollars or dong	Memory: Remember the revolution
The past	The future

The change from Saigon to Ho Chi Minh City is reflected in the difference between the generations. For older people, who always knew it as such, it is still Saigon, but for younger people it is Ho Chi Minh City, with a different mind-set and values system.

Many younger Vietnamese in Ho Chi Minh City have bought into consumer culture and have a different outlook on life than their parents and grandparents. The city described by Pico Iyer is certainly not the one that older generations knew. I saw many young women in Ho Chi Minh City with counterfeit black DKNY T-shirts, which were very popular, perhaps because fashion has become a global phenomenon.

It's ironic that a city named by the communists for their great national leader is now full of young men and women who have what might be described as a Western or bourgeois value system. Tourists are fortunate because, in a sense, they get the best of both versions of the city.

The food in Vietnam is very fresh and flavorful. Vietnamese cuisine is considered one of the great cuisines of the world.

Chapter 6

Exploring Vietnam's Culture:
Food and Entertainment

PHO

Pho, pronounced "fur," is a classic Vietnamese soup—generally eaten for breakfast but available all day long. It combines a rich beef or chicken stock with noodles, beef or chicken, vegetables, and lime juice. Some Vietnamese eat foods such as egg yolks with their *pho.* Thus, *pho* is a complete meal.

The stock is crucial. Beef *pho* is cooked for long hours with oxtails, marrow bones, onions, ginger, and other spices. This produces a very tasty and rich soup broth, to which hot noodles and beef or chicken are added when the *pho* is served to a customer. I would imagine that the Vietnamese learned a good deal about making rich broths from the French, who occupied the country for nearly 100 years. The dish originated in Hanoi and spread south to Ho Chi Minh City and then, as a result of Vietnamese migration, all over the world.

In an article titled "Looking Up an Old Love on the Streets of Vietnam," R. W. Apple describes, in rhapsodic terms, his passion for Vietnamese food and, in particular, for *pho,* which he suggests now has a "cult" status in Hanoi. *Pho* has, he suggests, "a unifying place in Vietnamese culture" (2003, p. D5). Apple points out that many cultures, such as the Japanese, eat soup to start the day. They start their day with miso; the Chinese have congee. So millions of people start the day with soup.

All through Vietnam one sees signs for *pho* or *pho/com* (rice). I've seen Vietnamese people in hotels eat fried eggs and omelets for breakfast, but most Vietnamese in the hotels I stayed in had either beef or chicken *pho* for breakfast, accompanied by bowls of vegetables or many other tasty foods.

Pho is to the Vietnamese what hamburgers and hot dogs are to Amercicans, except that *pho* is much healthier and a more complete meal. Wherever you are in Vietnam, you can get *pho*. I found that wherever I had it, it was delicious. It has curious parallels with the classic American breakfast:

Meal	American Breakfast	*Pho*
Starch	bread, cereal potatoes	noodles
Liquid	coffee, tea, milk	soup broth
Fruit and vegetables	orange juice	lime squeezed into *pho,* bean sprouts, basil, etc.
Protein	bacon, eggs	beef, chicken

Whereas the American breakfast (which seems to be based on the English one) has separate items and different courses, the Vietnamese breakfast has everything together in one bowl. In the United States, Vietnamese immigrants have adopted the American love of gigantism, and Vietnamese restaurants in America serve *pho* in huge bowls. These super-sized bowls of *pho* are accompanied by plates with greens, bean sprouts, and wedges of lime.

In recent years, because it is so fatty and high in calories, the so-called "classic" American breakfast of orange juice, cereal, bacon and eggs, pan-browned potatoes, and coffee has given way to high-protein vitamin bars and breakfast drinks, but *pho* retains its grip on the Vietnamese psyche and stomach. Whether this will remain the case for much longer is an interesting question.

If the cultural trends coming from Western European countries and the United States ever dislodge *pho* from the hearts and stomachs of the Vietnamese with vitamin bars or soft drinks (due to what some would call cultural imperialism or, more to the point, Coca-colonization), it will reflect a major change in the national psyche, and will also mean, at the very least, a great deal of new business for Vietnamese sign makers.

NUOC MAM (FISH SAUCE)

In Vietnamese "nuoc" means water and "mam" means salted fish. Nuoc mam is to Vietnamese food what soy sauce is to Chinese and Japanese food; nuoc mam can be considered, gastronomically speaking, a ubiquitous and universal agent. Combined with a number of different spices and herbs, nuoc mam is used to give Vietnamese food its distinctive quality. It is used as the base for many different sauces and flavors, some of which are wonderfully rich. Nuoc mam is made by putting layers of anchovies or other kinds of fish, salt, and various secret ingredients in large containers, often ceramic vats. The ingredients are then left to ferment for a few months or longer. The liquid on the bottom is then removed and poured back on the top of the container and left to ferment even more.

This process can be repeated many times, which means that nuoc mam, like wine, has different variations based on the kinds of fish, spices, and secret ingredients used, and the amount of time it is allowed to ferment. The first draining is considered the best; after that, water is poured into the barrel and a second and weaker nuoc mam is made. First drainings of nuoc mam are used for table dippings and later drainings are used for cooking. The best grade of nuoc mam is labeled *nhi* or *thuong hang*. Usually Americans aren't served nuoc mam in restaurants; it is believed they don't like the smell. They are served nuoc mam cham, a complex sauce made from nuoc mam, garlic, vinegar, sugar, chiles, and water that is sweet and more to the taste of tourists. Because it is based on nuoc mam instead of soy sauce, Vietnamese food isn't just a variation of Chinese food, although Chinese cooking, along with French, Thai, and Indian cooking, has obviously influenced Vietnamese cuisine.

What is interesting about nuoc mam is that it is salty but also somewhat sweet. This is not a combination that the American and Western European palate is used to; people in these regions are used to sweet-and-sour food (for example, pork) but don't, as a rule, eat food that is both sweet and salty. Someone once said that a genius is a person who can hold two contradictory beliefs at the same time. We could say that this is the genius of Vietnamese food, which is one of the biggest tourist attractions the country has to offer.

The Vietnamese, using nuoc mam in almost every dish they make, have created a truly superb cuisine; one that experts rank as an excellent, world-class cuisine, similar in status to French, Italian, Chinese, and Turkish cuisines. The spices Vietnamese chefs use and the various dipping sauces, most of which are built on a base of nuoc mam, play an important role in giving Vietnamese food its distinctive qualities.

VIETNAMESE METAL COFFEE POTS

When you order coffee in small restaurants in Vietnam, you will receive a cup or a glass on which you'll find a small metal coffee pot. It is actually a drip coffeemaker designed to make coffee for one person. It looks like a little stainless-steel tube or can, with a cover. On the bottom, there's a fine filter. The Vietnamese put some finely ground coffee in the bottom of the coffee pot and pour hot water into the pot. The hot water filters through the coffee grounds and drips into the cup. You get a small amount of very rich coffee. For people who don't like black coffee, the Vietnamese put some condensed milk in the bottom of the cup. This is called *ca phe sua da*. In Vietnamese restaurants in America, I've only seen this coffee served with ice; in Vietnam it is served hot or on ice.

Vietnam now exports a lot of coffee, though, I understand, it is generally of low or medium grade, and not the high-grade arabica that you find in the best coffees. I have two Vietnamese metal coffee-makers. When I want to recall the happy days I spent in Vietnam, drinking coffee in the hotels and little cafés there, I make myself some coffee Vietnamese style.

SPRING ROLLS

When people think of Vietnamese food, spring rolls might come to mind first. Spring rolls are appetizers, and only hint at the complexity of Vietnamese food. Spring rolls in the United States are usually served with nuoc mam cham, the complex and somewhat sweet sauce made of fish sauce, sugar, vinegar, lime, chiles, and garlic discussed earlier. I never had this sauce when I had spring rolls in Vietnam.

Vietnamese spring rolls are delicate, with a lovely texture and a very rich flavor. They are crunchy but also moist at the same time, one more example of the Vietnamese talent for combining opposites.

Somehow, they are not oily. This may be because they are made with rice-paper wrappers, which don't absorb oil, and because the Vietnamese generally fry their food in peanut oil rather than other oils that are heavier and greasier. (A variation of spring rolls that are not fried is also available.) Spring rolls are made with a number of different fillings, though usually it is some combination of ingredients such as minced pork, shrimp, crab, mushroom, edible fungus, onions, and bean sprouts. Some avant-garde Vietnamese restaurants put fish or chicken in them.

Although Vietnamese food, like Vietnamese culture, has been influenced by 1,000 years of domination by the Chinese and 100 years of control by the French, the Vietnamese still have been able to fashion a distinctive cuisine. Spring rolls are distant cousins to Chinese egg rolls, but like so many other aspects of Vietnamese culture, spring rolls are an adaptation that manage to have a unique identity all their own.

At the end of his article on Vietnamese food, R. W. Apple describes the way he and his wife feasted on spring rolls at Bun Cha Hang Manh, a restaurant in Hanoi that serves only two dishes: *bun cha,* a pork dish, and spring rolls. He describes the spring rolls: "Hang Manh's second dish is spring rolls (*nem ran* [italics added] in the north and *chia gio* [italics added] in the south)—great fat ones as thick as your thumb, packed with crab, ground pork, wood-ear mushrooms, onions and bean threads" (2003, p. D5). Apple noticed that the cooks at Hang Manh changed the fat every few minutes, which explained why the rolls there were so light and greaseless. Apple and his wife went to Hang Manh's twice and ate until they were stuffed.

A truly remarkable cuisine emerges from the pictures that Apple and numerous other writers paint of food in Vietnam. It is very easy, as I know from personal experience, for tourists in Vietnam to become "passionate eaters," similar to the Vietnamese themselves.

NON LA *(CONICAL HATS)*

Conical straw hats—in Vietnamese *non la*—are seen throughout Vietnam and are one of the most commonly recognized symbols of the country's culture. Literally speaking, *non la* means "hat of leaves." When you drive through Vietnam, wherever you go, you see women wearing these hats, working in the fields, driving motorbikes, selling things, and so on. *Non la* are certainly one of the most commonly recognized symbols or icons of Vietnamese culture.

These hats are sold in gift shops in Saigon for as little as 4,000 dong, though for 5,000 dong you get a better hat—that's approximately thirty-five cents, and they probably cost even less in markets. They are light, very strong, and some, such as those from Hue, have poems and other words in their linings. It is said that Vietnamese men often use the poems in these conical hats from Hue to gain insights into the character of the woman wearing the hat. They consider the poems in her hat as a reflection of her psyche and temperament.

An interesting fusion of practicality and aesthetics exists in these hats. Their design is simplicity itself: *non la* are flat cones with a diameter of approximately sixteen inches and a height of around eight inches. These hats are big, giving the wearer of a *non la* a certain physical presence. They have a strap to put under your chin to ensure they don't blow away. This combination of features produces a hat that costs almost nothing and is very light, strong, and large enough to protect one from the sun and rain. You also can use a conical hat as a fan, as it is stiff.

The Vietnamese conical hat is an icon that has attained a global reach and signifies, among other things, a country of farmers, who are probably most commonly identified with these hats. A hat of leaves suggests closeness to nature, and as you drive through Vietnam, you see many people in rice fields, up to their knees (or higher) in water, wearing these hats. Often the women wearing these hats have bandannas or masks over their faces; in Vietnam, having "light skin" is considered attractive, so the women try to protect themselves from the sun. This notion is very similar to the fashion in the United States, where the "tanned" look is no longer fashionable.

One of the most important qualities of the conical hat, as far as its symbolic power is concerned, it its utter simplicity. Egypt has the pyramids and Vietnam has the conical hat; both are basic geometric designs, though at opposite poles structurally speaking. And yet, in terms of their symbolic significance and cultural resonance, they are both remarkably powerful objects.

AO DAI:
THE TRADITIONAL VIETNAMESE COSTUME FOR WOMEN

The *ao dai* (pronounced âô zî in the north and âô yî in the south) is a women's garment that both covers everything and yet also reveals everything. That is because although it covers every part of a woman's body, it is very tight fitting, tailored so that it reveals the contours of a woman's body in great detail. It is a garment that does not flatter women who are not slender, but it is extremely flattering for a woman who has a good figure. It does not reveal cleavage, but it does show the contours of a woman's breasts.

An *ao dai* consists of a long-sleeved blouse with a high or boatneck that fits very tightly and has two long panels, on the front and the back. (The length of these panels varies, but they are often knee length.) It is generally worn over black or white trousers, which reach down to the ground. The *ao dai* is a variation of Chinese clothing that the Vietnamese adapted for their own purposes in the 1930s. Women with lower status, who work on farms and in lesser jobs, wear *ao ba bas,* a loose-fitting top and baggy pants.

From a psychoanalytic perspective, the *ao dai* can be thought of as a sexually revealing straitjacket, perhaps a distant relative of the priestly chalice in its similar shape and perhaps even, because it inhibits movement so much, a kind of chastity belt. I've always thought the women I saw wearing them, generally attractive young women who worked behind the desk in hotels or worked in fancy restaurants, looked uncomfortable in them. That may be a small price to pay for a fashion that is considered flattering. The *ao dai* emphasizes the body and directs attention to a woman's arms, breasts, and waist, but not her legs. Even though they cover a woman completely, because *ao dais* are often made by tailors and fit so snugly, they have the capacity to be sexy, without revealing cleavage or a well-turned leg.

In recent years *ao dais* have become a status symbol in Vietnam, and they are worn by young women who work in shops and by schoolgirls. *Ao dais* fell out of favor for about twenty or thirty years but are now making a comeback. Recently, "see-through" *ao dais,* with varying degrees of transparency, have achieved a measure of success, turning a garment that was designed to hide everything and also reveal a great deal into one that hides nothing and reveals everything.

The Internet hosts many Web sites that feature attractive young Vietnamese women, often with long hair cascading down to their waists, posing demurely, but sexily, in their *ao dais*. As with so many other items in Vietnam, the *ao dai* is a transformation of something borrowed from another culture and turned into something original. It also is one more example of what seems to be an important facet of Vietnamese culture—the unification of opposites.

HO CHI MINH'S BODY

Seeing Ho Chi Minh's body in the Ho Chi Minh Mausoleum was, I found, a rather ghoulish and chilling experience. It is one of the tourist experiences that just about everyone who visits Hanoi undergoes. Ho Chi Minh wanted to be cremated. But after he died, the Vietnamese political leaders believed that his body should be preserved and made available to the Vietnamese public, and others who might wish to see him, since he played such a pivotal role in Vietnamese history.

"Uncle Ho" to his followers, Ho Chi Minh can be called the father of his country and as such has a symbolic significance similar to that of George Washington in the United States. Ho Chi Minh was president of the Democratic Republic of Vietnam from 1946 until his death in 1969.

The way the Vietnamese have honored Ho Chi Minh is quite different from how the United States has honored George Washington. The United States erected a huge, thin tower to honor Washington. The Washington Monument towers over Washington, DC, providing wonderful views of the city.

In Vietnam, the focus is on Ho Chi Minh's body, on Ho as a person. He is kept in a state of preservation in an airtight glass casket. At first, the Vietnamese had to ship Ho's body back to Russia every few years for some kind of renewal treatment, but in recent years the Vietnamese have learned to maintain his body on their own. He lies, preserved somehow, in the casket, a triumph of the undertaker's art.

When you go to the museum where Ho's body is housed, you cannot help but be affected by the reverence with which the Vietnamese, who file past his body in an endless stream, treat seeing his body. It appears to be important to them to see Ho Chi Minh, even if he's dead and preserved under glass like a specimen in a science museum. The reason Ho Chi Minh's body is preserved in an airtight container may also have something to do with Vietnamese culture and the Vietnamese religious sensibility, which advocates honoring the dead and keeping them near their living descendants.

A guide told me that the Vietnamese bury their dead twice. First, immediately after a person dies, he or she is buried. Then, several years later the bones are dug up and brought to where the person originally grew up. Here they are buried again, often with elaborate gravestones. In the United States, we bury people (or cremate them) and put up, generally speaking, relatively simple gravestones to honor them. We name buildings and cities after our dead leaders. The Vietnamese did the same thing when they changed the name of Saigon to Ho Chi Minh City.

Seeing Ho Chi Minh, lying there serenely in his glass casket, you don't get any sense of the turbulent life he led and the epic struggles he went through in his goal to create a united Vietnam. In his earlier years he traveled the world; he spent time in Paris, the United States, and a number of other countries before he returned to his home country. When he returned in 1941 he founded the Communist Party of Vietnam and led a revolution that would eventuate in a unified country based on communist (officially, at least) principles.

Ho Chi Minh had many aliases; it is estimated that he used about fifty different names over the years. His birth name was Nguyen Tat Thanh. Ho Chi Minh spent thirty years working in a variety of jobs, away from the country he loved. When he came back, he shook the world; he led a revolution and founded a new nation, emerging as one of the most well-known leaders of the twentieth century.

GENERAL GIAP:
THE SNOW-COVERED VOLCANO

Vo Nguyen Giap doesn't get as much attention in Vietnam as Ho Chi Minh. No city is named after him, and his face is not on Vietnamese money, the way Ho Chi Minh's is. However, it is fair to say that General Giap played a major role in the emergence of Vietnam as an independent nation and that his role was almost as important as Ho Chi Minh's.

Vo Nguyen Giap was born on August 25, 1911. He attended the same high school as Ho Chi Minh, and went through the university system in Vietnam, earning a law degree in 1937. He then became a professor of history. He married a woman named Quant Thai and they had a child, who Giap named Hang Anh, which means "red queen of flowers."

Giap left his teaching post, surreptitiously, to escape to China, where he became connected with the Vietminh. The French Deuxième Bureau arrested his wife when they found out that Giap was missing, and sent her to Hao Lo Prison ("the oven") which later became the infamous Hanoi Hilton. She was imprisoned and tortured there, and died a few years later. The French claimed she committed suicide; this theory is disputed by others who say she was tortured to death. Another member of Giap's family, his sister-in law, was guillotined by the French.

Giap was a self-taught military strategist and logistics expert who learned a great deal from his experiences fighting in the field. He also was a military genius who was able to defeat two first world armies with relatively weak third world ones. In 1953, a French general, Henri Navarre, fortified the valley of Dien Bien Phu in northwestern Vietnam with twelve battalions of French soldiers. Navarre assumed that he would draw the Vietnamese army into a large-scale battle there, where conditions would be favorable for his soldiers.

Giap decided against doing this, even though he had thirty-three battalions of infantry soldiers and six regiments of artillery men. Instead, he transported artillery pieces by porter through dense jungles and placed his artillery on the hills around Dien Bien Phu. With his artillery, he hammered the French troops. The French parachuted six more battalions of soldiers into Dien Bien Phu as the military situation worsened. Giap also surrounded the French troops and was able to prevent French reinforcements from arriving. On May 6, 1954, the Vietnamese army took Dien Bien Phu, with a loss of 25,000 troops, and had captured or killed an estimated 16,000 French troops.

Giap described this victory as "a great and first victory of a feudal colonial nation, whose agricultural economy is backward, against the great imperialist capitalist [country] which has a modern industry and a great army" (CNN, 1996). He also predicted that Vietnam would eventually find itself in a conflict with America, a conflict he was certain Vietnam would win. As he said about American involvement,

"They did not know the limits of power. . . . No matter how powerful you are there are certain limits and they did not understand it well."

Giap also was the mastermind behind the Vietcong forces in the "American War," as it is known in Vietnam, and the Tet Offensive. This series of battles led to America leaving Vietnam in 1973. Two years later South Vietnam fell to General Giap's troops and the nation was unified.

Giap was called the "snow-covered volcano" because of his volatile temper. But he had another side. He was a poet, and wrote the following lovely haiku-like poems:

> Talents were like leaves in the autumn
> and heroes appeared like the dawn.

and

> When a herdsman played his flute,
> the moon rose higher in the sky.

If you're going to lead a war for national independence, as Ho Chi Minh did, it helps to have a military genius such as Vo Nguyen Giap on your side.

GREEN PITH HELMETS

In the northern half of Vietnam, large numbers of men wear green pith helmets, similar to those the Vietcong soldiers wore in the American/Vietnam War. In the southern half of the country, from Da Nang south, few men wear them. These helmets symbolize, among other things, the pride the Vietnamese have in their history of triumph in wars of national liberation, especially in the war between the Vietcong and the United States.

The Vietnamese have fought, and defeated, the Mongols, the Chinese army, the French army, and the U.S. army. So these green pith helmets are signifiers of Vietnamese military prowess and independence, and of Vietnamese memory. The helmets are not heavy, though they weigh a good deal more than conical hats. The helmets also weigh much less than American metal helmets do, and don't provide as much protection as American helmets did.

American troops, weighed down by their helmets, heavy boots, and other essential gear, struggled in the terrible heat and humidity of Vietnam. The American soldiers had boots and the Vietnamese wore flip-flops. The United States had the technology and the Vietnamese had the will.

When I was on Cat Ba Island with a group of tourists, I had an experience that symbolized, in a way, the confrontation between Vietnam and the United States and other first world nations. We were all on a trek, but some people, myself included, decided to take only the easy part, and remain at a lovely outdoor restaurant in a small village while those who wished to do so climbed a very steep hill. The climb would take a couple of hours and was, we were told, a very difficult and strenuous hike. Five or six younger members of our group, men and women in their thirties, decided to climb the hill. I recall seeing them put on heavy socks and lace up huge, very rugged, hiking boots in preparation for the trek. When the Vietnamese guide came to lead the hike, I was astounded; he was wearing flip-flops.

Heavy boots and flip-flops. They symbolized, in a rather extreme manner, the difference between the American military machine and the Vietnamese one (not to suggest that the Vietnamese didn't have tanks, howitzers, and other heavy-duty military arms). The Vietnamese developed ways of carrying as much as 500 pounds of military equipment on bikes and wheeled these bikes along the Ho Chi Minh Trail. The United States spent billions of dollars on a high-tech military machine, and the most advanced military force in the world was defeated by a third world army of soldiers wearing green pith helmets and flip-flops, while wheeling bicycles and digging tunnels.

We do not choose symbols on rational grounds all the time. Vietnamese men can wear any number of different kinds of straw hats that have wide brims and protect them from the sun better than the pith helmets do, but straw hats don't convey the same message for men in the northern half of Vietnam that the green pith helmets do. In the southern half of Vietnam, where the memory of the war is different, and where many Vietnamese worked for the United States Army, these green pith helmets understandably are not very popular.

CU CHI TUNNELS

The Cu Chi Tunnels are one of the most popular tourist attractions in Vietnam, and are generally part of a day trip from Saigon that starts with a three-hour bus ride to attend the noon services at the Cao Dai Cathedral. The tunnels are nearby. In 1940, the anticolonial Vietminh army dug storage areas for their arms near Cu Chi. Later they realized that the tunnels also could be used to hide troops. These storage areas eventually became, over a decade, 250 kilometers (about 150 miles) of small (approximately two feet wide and six feet deep) tunnels that enabled the Vietcong to move into Saigon whenever they wished. Some of the tunnels even went under an American army base.

These tunnels evolved into a system of underground dormitories, meeting rooms, and hospitals, but they were very hot and spending time in them was difficult. The Vietcong soldiers also had to contend with snakes, scorpions, and many other hazards. To accomodate tourists from Western countries, whose body frames are larger than those of the Vietnamese, the Vietnamese government enlarged several hundred feet of the tunnels. I decided to go into the tunnels, but when I walked down a stairway leading into them, it was so hot and oppressive and the air so stale, that I turned back.

When you go to visit the tunnels, you are subjected to a short video that is very primitive and is obviously a bit of heavy-handed Vietnamese propaganda. Then the guides take you to an area where they show a half-dozen different devices that the Vietcong put in the traps they dug for American troops and their allies. They would dig pits and put various kinds of devices with poison spikes in them. Some of the devices were designed with barbs so they couldn't be taken out of a person's leg without having to take the entire device and the afflicted soldier to a hospital. The Vietcong also tied trip wires along paths that, when triggered, would cause small land mines to explode.

Seeing the row of ingenious and terrifying devices the Vietcong invented was horrendous. But wars are not pleasant, and the devices were quite primitive when compared to what the Americans had: bombs, napalm, and Agent Orange, for example.

CD CAFÉS

CD cafés are in all the big cities. These are places where you can get almost any music on a compact disc (and all the new computer programs from Microsoft and other companies) at incredible prices. That's because they are all pirated copies of CDs. When one legitimate CD is purchased by someone, somewhere in Vietnam, before you know it, pirated copies become available all over the country. The CD café I went to in Saigon must have had 10,000 or 20,000 compact discs. None were in clear plastic jewel cases; they were all in paper envelopes.

The Vietnamese also copy books. They are masters at offset printing; when you dine in restaurants in some of the larger cities, it isn't unusual for men and women, with a stack of Lonely Planet guides, to ask if you wish to buy any books. You can tell the pirated versions from the real Lonely Planet books because the pirated versions don't have shiny covers. I would imagine that many other pirated books, of all kinds, are available as well.

Something interesting happened when I went into one CD café and looked for an Edith Piaf CD. I looked under "P," which is how they would be placed in America and, quite likely, most other countries. I didn't find any of her CDs in the stacks.

A clerk came over to me as I was rummaging through the section and asked me what I was looking for. I told him, and he then turned and went to the "E" section and pulled out three different CDs of Piaf's.

This brought to mind problems I'd had with Vietnamese names, for I was never sure (until someone explained the naming system to me) what was someone's first, middle, or last name. It turns out that the Vietnamese classify CDs by the first names of the artists. I found that astonishing, but, if you think about it, logical. In much of Asia, the last name is given first, so it was logical for the clerks in the CD café to put a disk by Edith Piaf in the "E" section. For the Vietnamese, Edith would be seen as the family name. Those in the United States think that last names are critical, since many people can have the same first name. There are many Ediths, but few Piafs.

I purchased one CD, *Padam . . . Padam.* It had a sticker on it saying "Mfd. for BMG. Direct Marketing Is Under License." This would suggest the company had an arrangement with BMG to copy the CD.

That is possible, but hardly likely. The CD cost 12,000 dong, which is about eighty-four cents. At that price I had doubts about whether it would work, but when I listened to it, it was perfect.

I must admit that I don't feel a sense of moral outrage at the piracy that goes on in Vietnam. Vietnam is a very poor country and most of the Vietnamese people have very little money. By Vietnamese standards, of course, the CD was expensive. Assuming that the average national salary is about 400 dollars a year, the price of my CD represents half a day's wages.

DONG AND DOLLARS

If you don't have Vietnamese dong, you can pay for most things in Vietnam with American dollars. You can't use dollars to buy produce from street vendors, as a rule, because the price of what they are selling is so low. However, you can use dollars in most restaurants and in most shops. This tells you much about contemporary Vietnam, for with dong and dollars we find the same split personality that we find in the Saigon and Ho Chi Minh City dualism. The American presence is still strong, at the currency level if not so in many other places. The late president of Vietnam, Ho Chi Minh, on Vietnamese dong, and the first American president, George Washington, represented on the dollar, become substitutes for one another at the currency level.

The Vietnamese unit of currency is the dong. No coins are used.

How ironic. Especially so since Ho didn't want to have his face put on the dong, just as he didn't want his body to be preserved and placed in a mausoleum for all to see.

All dong have Ho Chi Minh's picture on them, and all bills are the same size, but they differ in color. The American dollar is worth approximately 15,000 dong, which means if you cash a $100 traveler's check, you become an instant "dong millionaire." On my first day in Hanoi, I went to an ATM and purchased 2 million dong. It cost me $134. The dong came in 50,000-dong bills, so I got a stack of forty of them.

As I traveled through Vietnam, I had occasion to break the 50,000-dong bills, which meant I often had a stack of 500-dong bills, 1,000-dong bills, 2,000-dong bills, 5,000-dong bills, 10,000-dong bills, and 20,000-dong bills in addition to my 50,000-dong bills. It is not unusual to carry a thick wad of dong with you, and you need them. Coins do not exist in Vietnam. But a 1,000-dong bill is worth only around seven cents.

The capitalist ethos has now spread all over the world, and in Vietnam, despite its official socialist rhetoric, capitalism prevails. The American military may be gone but, in interesting ways, through the dollars that change hands so frequently in Vietnam, an American presence lingers on.

ROI NUOC *(WATER PUPPETS)*

Roi nuoc, or water puppetry, a uniquely Vietnamese art form, reflects a number of interesting facets of Vietnamese culture and psyche. The water puppetry show I saw, which lasted about one hour and had a number of relatively short acts, was very amusing. You could see the Vietnamese sense of humor showing through in the puppets that were used and in the way the puppets related to one another. The humor was light and ebullient.

The evening began with a short concert by the musicians who accompanied the puppet show. Then the puppets made their appearance. Most of the acts were taken from folklore and one showed such puppets as lions, fishermen, fish, dragons, and turtles cavorting and splashing around in the water. One scene—a very elaborate parade with a large number of puppets—had an element of grandeur about it.

The amount of effort and the skill needed to stage that parade was remarkable.

The Vietnamese have been doing water puppetry for 1,000 years, so they've had a lot of time to perfect their technique. Originally it was developed by farmers in the Red River Delta. Water creates difficulties for puppeteers, but also hides the rods and strings they use. In addition, they can use the powers of water—splashes and rippling effects—for their own purposes. Puppetry also reflects, I would suggest, the power of water in the Vietnamese psyche. Vietnam is the second-largest exporter of rice (after Thailand), and rice is a grain that is grown in water. Wherever you go in Vietnam, you're seldom far from water; it seems there always is a river or waterfall, or a sea.

Water puppetry is not an advanced art form, as are opera or ballet. It is a vernacular art, a popular art, and has an element of innocence and simplicity about it. You can deal with any topics you choose in a puppet show; the art form is not, by its nature, limited to legends or portrayals of life in villages. However, puppetry traditionally has tended to deal with everyday matters in a light tone.

The difficulties posed by staging a puppet show in water are considerable. The puppeteers have to stand in water up to their chests (they wear rubber waders now) and manipulate twenty-pound puppets on fifteen-foot rods. They also use strings to move upper-body parts and create facial expressions. Sometimes it takes three puppeteers to handle one puppet. The puppets themselves are about two feet high.

Water puppetry reflects its ingenuity. Figuring out how to move these puppets and make them "lifelike" takes a lot of resourcefulness. The various troupes of water puppeteers guard their methods and techniques. It takes a number of years for a person to learn the art of water puppetry. This unique and charming art reflects the lighter side of the Vietnamese psyche.

Halong Bay is a spectacularly beautiful body of water that has been declared a World Heritage Site by UNESCO.

Pictured here is a small Tay village market about one hour north of Hanoi that serves the local villagers. Most of these women wear either blue or purple clothing with the traditional conical hats.

This image shows the enormous amount of work involved in growing rice. The Vietnamese farmers make use of every bit of space.

There's always a great deal of traffic in the Mekong Delta, where the floating markets are a very popular tourist attraction.

Along the Mekong Delta, about three hours south of Saigon, you see many different kinds of homes. Homes such as this one are commonly seen in the Mekong, where the climate is sultry and there is little need for protection from the elements.

A typical scene in Hanoi: Men riding their bicycles—or walking beside them because the bikes are loaded with goods to sell. Pith helmets are popular in the northern parts of Vietnam.

The Red Zhao are one of the traditional ethnic groups of northern Vietnam. A number of them are located in small villages in and around Sapa, where they sell trinkets and other items.

The central market in Sapa is full of beautiful fruits and vegetables.

The Black Hmong live in northern Vietnam. Like the Red Zhao, they are aggressive marketers and have many items for sale. Their clothes are made of hemp, a heavy cloth woven by hand. This hemp clothing is worn in many layers. Visitors will notice that the hands of many Black Hmong are tinted blue; this stems from their routine use of indigo dye in cloth making.

These girls live in a rural area about an hour from Sapa. They come to town daily to sell small items, such as bracelets, bags, and earrings.

Many buildings in Vietnam show the influence of the French, who occupied the country for a number of years. Houses are often painted in shades of yellow and green.

This is a typical vista in northern Vietnam around the Sapa area and even further west. The country is marked by steep hills covered by rice fields. The views are breathtaking.

PART IV:
REMEMBERING VIETNAM—
BACK IN THE UNITED STATES

History weighs heavily on Vietnam. For more than a decade, reportage of the war that racked this slender country portrayed it as a netherworld of savagery and slaughter, and even after the American War ended it was further pigeon-holed by Hollywood's seamless chain of combat movies. Yet, only twenty-odd years after the war's end, this incredibly resilient nation is beginning to emerge from the shadows: access is now easier than ever, and the country has reinvented its old-style communist system as a free market economy that encourages contact. As the number of tourists finding their way here soars, the word is out that this is a land not of bomb craters and army ordnance, but of shimmering paddy fields and sugar-white beaches, full-tilt cities and venerable pagodas—often overwhelming in its sheer beauty.

Jan Dodd and Mark Lewis,
The Rough Guide to Vietnam (Third Edition)

Concepts are purely differential and defined not by their positive content but negatively by their relations with the other terms of the system. Their most precise characteristic is in being what the others are not. . . . Signs function, then, not through their intrinsic value but through their relative position.

Ferdinand de Saussure,
Course in General Linguistics

Pictured here is one of the most colorful fruits found in Vietnam, the dragon fruit. It's sold on every street corner in town during its peak harvest season. For many Westerners, this fruit is an acquired taste.

Chapter 7

Reflections on Touring Vietnam

We suffered from jet lag for more than two weeks after returning from Vietnam. I found myself, at times, eating a snack at 3:30 a.m., due to having slept at odd times during the day and night. I had brought back some wonderful Vietnamese candy (chewy nougats with sesame seeds and rice crackers with sesame seeds), so I still was able to have a taste of Vietnam weeks after I returned. I also purchased a pound of very fine Vietnamese coffee, which I made every day. It is curious how certain tastes linger in your memory.

A JUMBLE OF MEMORIES

We arrived in Hanoi on Friday, June 29, after a fifteen-hour flight to Hong Kong, an eight-hour wait in the Hong Kong International Airport, and a short ninety-minute flight from Hong Kong to Hanoi. Getting to Hanoi isn't easy; most of the flights to Vietnam, so it seems, go to Ho Chi Minh City. A guide and a driver, sent by our tour company, met my wife and I at the airport.

They took us to the Salute Hotel. It's a so-called mini-hotel located just a few hundred feet from Hoan Kiem Lake, which is in the center of the old city, and just around the corner from the water puppet theater. The Salute is a small hotel, with about a dozen rooms, but it is quite modern and has a very friendly staff. Every morning, when we went down for breakfast, two beautiful young women in *ao dais*, greeted us with big smiles. They also taught us a few Vietnamese words.

I was to give two lectures/readings in Hanoi, one at an institute of library study and the other at a school of foreign affairs, on Monday, July 2, the first day of our tour, when I had nothing else scheduled. One of my lectures was on postmodernism. I read from my mystery,

Postmortem for a Postmodernist, and talked about writing the book and about postmodernism. A lively hour-long discussion period followed, during which I answered questions that the professors and journalists had written down and passed to my interpreter.

I had earlier e-mailed the passages from the book that I would be reading and the interpreter had translated them into Vietnamese and duplicated them. So the people in my audience could read the material from my book in Vietnamese, which helped a great deal. About twenty-five or thirty people attended the reading; they asked excellent questions. I left a copy of the book for the library at the institute. My interpreter was very animated and did a good job of trying to catch the spirit of my answers.

Having an interpreter/translator was a big help, but it also cut down on the amount of material I could deal with. I did the best I could. As I read from my book I could only wonder what the members of the audience were thinking. I chose some passages that were didactic in tone, so my audience members could see how I used the narrative form, a zany comic academic mystery story, to teach readers something about postmodernism.

My second lecture was on my analysis of everyday life in the United States. I brought a copy of my book, *Bloom's Morning,* and read passages from it about king-sized beds, master bedrooms, and trash compactors. Everyone in this group understood English, so I didn't need a translator. The woman who introduced me, a professor of international relations, used the term postmodern in discussing the topic.

"Had I known you were interested in postmodernism," I said, "I could have given my morning lecture here."

A woman in the group asked me if *Bloom's Morning* was a novel, which struck me as quite interesting. I hadn't thought of my book as a work of fiction; but its name's connection to Bloom in Joyce's *Ulysses* must have caused her to see it that way.

That evening my wife and I went out for dinner to the Little Hanoi, a small restaurant frequented by tourists. I can recall, almost as if I were there right now, the taste of a fabulous dish of roast pork with a very rich and complex chili sauce we had that night. I can well understand Proust's use of a madeleine in his novel *Remembrance of Things Past,* for food does have the power to give you remembrances of meals past and times past.

I had some clothes made in Hoi An, and often wear a pair of black nylon pants I got there. The tailor said, "I will make the pants a bit short so you won't fall. You are an old man and must be careful. I don't want you to trip over my pants." I also had a suit made, which fits beautifully. I often wear a handsome cloth hat I bought in Sapa from an elderly Black Hmong lady.

I have many photographs from Vietnam. It's curious how images resonate in your mind and you can recall being at a particular place when you took the photograph. Some tourism scholars have argued that tourism essentially involves "consuming" images, what they call "the tourist gaze." As John Urry, a British sociologist who has done important work on tourism, writes in an update of his ideas in a recent Internet paper, the tourist gaze has now become global. His article, "Globalizing the Tourist Gaze" considers how important globalization has become for tourism. He writes that when he published his book *The Tourist Gaze* in 1990, it was unclear "how significant the processes we now call 'globalisation' were to become" (<www.comp.lancs.ac.uk/sociology/soc079ju.html>). Urry explains that a number of new developments have taken tourism, which formerly existed at the margins of the new global order, and placed it squarely in the center of the world economy. It also has become, in recent years, a subject of considerable interest to academics and is assuming a place of considerable importance in the scholarly world. Urry writes:

> First, tourism infrastructures have been constructed in what would have been thought of as the unlikeliest of places. . . . Further, there are large increases in the growth of tourists emanating from very different countries, especially those of the "orient," that once were places visited and consumed by those *from* the "west." . . . Moreover, many types of work are now found with these circuits of global tourism. It is difficult not to be implicated within, or affected by, one or more of these circuits that increasingly overlap with a more general "economy of signs" spreading across multiple spaces of consumption (Lash and Urry, 1994). (<www.comp.lancs.ac.uk/sociology/soc079ju.html>)

As Urry points out, few places, anywhere in the world, have not been affected, either directly or indirectly, by the development of global tourism. As he explains, images and icons dominate our experience as tourists. What Urry calls "vernacular" icons was the focus in my analysis of "semiotic" Vietnam.

I can vividly remember the ride from the airport in Hanoi to the downtown area. You pass by fields where peasants are working and the landscape is incredibly green. Then, in about a half hour, you're in Hanoi and the motorbike riders are swarming all over the roads. I always marveled at the skill of the tour drivers as they cut through the endless parade of motorbikes, buses, and trucks that filled the streets. Many of the drivers knew a lot more English than they let on. We finally realized this when we asked them, so we could talk with them when, for example, they were taking us to an airport and we weren't with a guide.

Except for our stay in Sapa and our trip to Halong Bay, we were with different guides each day. They all had different styles. In Hue, our guide was a lovely woman, the wife of a physician. She wore a beautiful *ao dai,* with long sleeves and a high neck, though it was an incredibly hot day. She brought my wife a beautiful bouquet of flowers. I sympathized with her, taking tourists to the same places day after day, but relatively speaking, I believe being a guide is a good job. She only led tours in Hue, because she had two small children to take care of. I wondered about the burnout rate of guides. One of my guides talked about being exhausted and stressed out, and I can understand why.

Besides the boredom of doing the same thing, day after day, week after week, guides also must physically exert themselves. I'm thinking of the hard-sleeper train from Hanoi to Lao Cai, which takes ten hours, the two-hour ride to Sapa from Lao Cai, the six-hour jeep ride (three hours each way on extremely bumpy roads) to visit the Sunday market, and the seven-hour trek to the hill-tribes villages that many people take. My wife and I didn't take the trek because we were very tired, so our guide was lucky and had the day off. To get back to Hanoi, you have another ride to Lao Cai and another ten-hour train trip to Hanoi, getting in at 4:45 a.m., no less. We had a free day when we got back to Hanoi to recuperate from the ordeal, but I don't think our guide did. Our guides told us that they work seven days a week and may take one day off a month. The Vietnamese are a very hardworking people. However, they seem to be in good spirits, laughing very often.

I had thought that women doing construction work, who wore cloth masks over their noses and the bottoms of their faces, did so to protect themselves from dust. I learned that they actually wore these masks to keep their skin light. Many women in Vietnam wear bandannas or masks of some kind, while they labor in the fields, dig ditches, or load trucks with dirt in the cities. Women in Vietnam do much more manual labor than woman in the United States.

When I saw women with cloth masks, and only their eyes showing, especially when they were on motorbikes, I couldn't help but think I was in the Wild West, watching bandits and outlaws riding into town. Often, the motorbike drivers have one, two, or three other people on their bikes with them. I realized I was in a kind of Wild West, except that it was in southeastern Asia. Other similarities may exist between Vietnam now and the Wild West. They both have the grandeur of the scenery, except in Vietnam the grandeur isn't from mountains (except near Sapa in the northwest) but from the beautiful fields of rice and vegetables, and from the palm trees and the Mekong river snaking everywhere throughout the Mekong Delta.

I remember fondly the boats we took there, most of them looking as if they might fall apart any minute. On our tour, we had occasion to climb in and out of more than a dozen boats, of all sizes. In one day we might be in a small rowboat that could hold four people, a long motorized boat that could hold eight or ten people, and a large motorboat that could hold fifty people. The boats weren't fancy, but they got the job done. As I sat in a boat and looked out, I saw many other boats, of all kinds, sailing here and there. We did see some boatyards where workers were building new boats. It was really quite remarkable how the Vietnamese boatbuilders created them with only simple tools.

In one boat, on the way back to Hoi An from visiting Champa ruins, we were given a lunch: a simple sandwich, some sticky rice in a banana leaf, a bottle of water, and a large piece of pineapple. It was cool in the middle of the river and the lunch was delicious. We had worked up an appetite wandering around My Son, where the Champa ruins are located. That day was one of the hottest days we spent in Vietnam.

That night, at about six o'clock, all the lights in the town suddenly went out. The electrical system had shut down. It flickered on and off from time to time, for a few minutes, but stayed off until around ten o'clock at night. Our hotel had a generator, which kept the lights on, but wasn't powerful enough to operate the air conditioner. I had to

Pool is a very popular pastime in Vietnam. Well-used pool tables can be found in most rural and urban areas throughout the country.

pay a woman at a cloth (tailor) shop for some suits that had been made for us, and ended up paying her by candlelight.

Just when we were prepared to go to bed, in a room that was very hot, the electricity was restored and we were "saved." We were in a very nice hotel in Hoi An, The Vinh Hung 2, which boasts a lovely swimming pool. I spent a lot of time in that pool, after tours and at various other times, when I could sneak some free time.

We only passed through Da Nang. It is not considered a particularly interesting city, though many tourists stop there to see the Cham Museum. Da Nang had many more bicyclists than other cities. We had a mid-morning flight and left our hotel in Hoi An for the airport after an early breakfast, at around 7:00 a.m. The streets were full of people on bicycles and motorbikes, going to work. The terrain is very flat so it is easy to travel by bicycle. Men sat in cafés drinking coffee. Women with little carts sold baguettes, which they would fill with pâté for a few thousand dong.

The Da Nang International Airport is small because there's not much air traffic to the city. We flew to Ho Chi Minh City, and by noon we were in the Vien Dong Hotel (a moderately priced hotel by American standards), in Pham Ngu Lao, the backpacker section of the city. The sidewalks were wider and not crowded as they were in Hanoi. I was pleasantly surprised. Ho Chi Minh City/Saigon is different from Hoi An, for the latter is a small town and you can walk to everything in it. Ho Chi Minh City, on the other hand, is a gigantic place. Except when we were on our tour, being shown the city by a guide with a driver, we stayed close to our hotel, which had a lovely breakfast buffet on the tenth floor. You could look out over the downtown section of Ho Chi Minh City as you drank your pineapple juice, ate your baguette and omelet, sampled dim sum, and feasted on pineapple and other melons. The coffee, alas, was American style, served in a big carafe.

THE ACTUAL VIETNAM
VERSUS THE VIRTUAL VIETNAM

There's a lot of laughter in Vietnam, and I found that very heartening. Of course, as one might suspect, the actual Vietnam was quite different from the Vietnam I had imagined from reading tour books and other books about the country. I found a country that was spectacularly beautiful, with lush green vistas, full of warm and friendly people.

Fortunately, we didn't meet up with any of the criminals we'd been warned about racing about on motorbikes and snatching jewelry, cameras, and glasses off the faces of unsuspecting tourists. We were never surrounded by mobs of children whose mothers used them to divert our attention so they could pick our pockets. The average person in Vietnam makes approximately 20,000 dong per day, or $400 a year. On that salary, the people are able to eat various goodies in small sidewalk restaurants, drink beer in inexpensive *bia hoi* beer halls, and ride around on Honda motorbikes (or Chinese imitations for those who can't afford Hondas). Honda motorbikes cost about $2,000; Chinese imitations cost around $600, but they are not made as well. In the big cities people earn more money, but the cost of living is also greater.

We didn't get sick, either. The food in Vietnam is excellent; even little restaurants in small villages serve delicious food. I don't think you can get a bad bowl of soup in the country, and you can get a very good bowl of soup with bean curd for 5,000 dong (35 cents) in a small restaurant we dined at in Hanoi. We had a marvelous bowl of noodle soup in a bustling restaurant in Chau Doc for 8,000 dong each. When I asked for the menu, they didn't have any. A waitress brought me to the kitchen area, right in the middle of the restaurant, where cooks were frenetically adding noodles and dumplings to steaming bowls of soup. I pointed to one of the bowls and raised two fingers to indicate we wanted two bowls of soup. It had noodles, a rich broth, and wonton dumplings, and it came with a small dessert (some kind of pudding). We had a bottle of soda for an additional 3,000 dong each, which meant my wife and I had a lovely dinner for 22,000 dong, which is about $1.50.

The guidebooks tell you about the motorbikes on the streets, but they can't prepare you for the chaos you experience on the streets of Hanoi, where thousands of Vietnamese motorbikes clog the streets, drivers all honking their horns furiously. Just crossing the street in Hanoi is an exciting and somewhat dangerous adventure, especially because there are few stoplights. In addition, the Vietnamese don't pay much attention to the stoplights, running red lights with abandon.

Of course, I was always in a hotel in a tourist area, so my experiences in Hanoi and Ho Chi Minh City were not typical, perhaps. But no matter where you stay in these cities, especially at rush hour, swarms of motorbikers can be seen, along with people on bicycles, pedicab drivers, cars, and trucks; it is a truly spectacular and somewhat terrifying sight. I was told by our guides that when we wanted to cross the street, to walk slowly and not stop, so the people on their motorbikes could gage how to avoid hitting us. I must confess that sometimes I froze, and, many times, had very close calls, and barely avoided being hit. Many of the countries in southeast Asia are full of motorbikes, so Vietnam is not unusual in that respect.

STREET CULTURES AND HOUSE CULTURES

Vietnam, similar to a number of other Asian countries, has what might be called a street culture; that is, a good deal of life is lived on the streets of Vietnam, in contrast to a country such as the United States, which I would describe as essentially a house culture. The difference between the two can be seen in the list that follows.

Vietnam	United States
Street culture	House culture
Hanoi	Mill Valley, California
People everywhere	People sequestered
Noisy	Quiet
City	Suburbs
Togetherness	Isolation
Public eating	Private eating
Anomie	Alienation

These oppositions are, perhaps, somewhat forced, but I think you can see the difference between a culture in which so much takes place on the street (at least in the cities) and one in which so much takes place at home, in one's house. By six o'clock in the morning, the streets of Hanoi and other cities are full of people—cooking away, eating in the numerous restaurants, sitting in cafés and having coffee, selling baguettes, and riding to work on motorbikes. By seven the motorbikes are like gigantic dense swarms of fish, flowing through the streets. Noise and bustling activity abound.

I think the experience of being in a city with a great deal of life on the street is appealing to people who come from "home" cultures, where people live in relative isolation without the excitement and vitality that can be found in street cultures.

The Vietnamese motorbikers don't pay much attention to stoplights or rules, so one of my guides informed me. That leads me to suggest that the Vietnamese tend to be *anomic* rather than *alienated*, which seems to be more of a problem in Western European and U.S. society.

I have used the rather extreme polar opposites Hanoi and Mill Valley to make a point. In Hanoi, the action is on the streets, while in suburbs such as Mill Valley, where I live, the center of life is the house. Much of what I say about Mill Valley could be said about San Francisco, and many other places in the United States and large portions of Western Europe. People drive their cars up to their houses and push a button, the garage door opens, and they drive into their garages. Then the garage door closes, and you might not see them again that day.

As a rule, you hardly see anyone on the streets in most of Mill Valley, except gardeners, tradespeople (contractors fixing houses), joggers, and people walking their dogs. You can, I should point out, find people shopping and eating in restaurants in the downtown "tourist" section. San Francisco has more action, but even in that city, except for a few areas with restaurants and nightlife, is almost deserted in the evenings. In downtown Hanoi and Ho Chi Minh City, people are out relatively late into the night.

One question I face, as I analyze Vietnam, is: What is distinctive and unique to Vietnam? It is a question that the Vietnamese, no doubt, have thought about for many centuries, wedged in, as they are, between two giant countries (China and India), whose cultures have influenced them greatly over the past 1,000 years.

AN AGE-OLD QUESTION

One morning a member of the hotel staff, who opened doors to the breakfast room, asked me a question.

"Sir," he said, "could you please tell me how old you are?"

"Thirty-nine," I said.

He laughed.

"I'm really sixty-eight," I said.

"I would have guessed that you were ten years younger," he said.

His question wasn't unusual. My wife and I met many people in Vietnam who commented on our ages, as if my being sixty-eight was a curiosity. Maybe it is because the life expectancy for men in Vietnam is not very high (only 67.58 years) or that elderly people don't travel very much. Being "old," or more precisely, being considered old, meant that my wife and I got the best cabin on our boat at Halong Bay and I got short black pants.

It was strange, but not unpleasant, being in a country where people are honored and given respect for being elderly. Before going to Vietnam I had never thought of myself as old, and I still don't. Many people think of themselves as fifteen or twenty years younger than they actually are, and I'm no exception. So it was quite a shock to be continually reminded of my age and being shown respect as someone "elderly." (I'll never forget the shock I had when I turned sixty-five and got a letter from the government classifying me as "elderly retired.") Now that we are back in the United States, my wife and I have reverted to thinking of ourselves as middle-aged.

One's memory of a trip is always a jumble. At one moment, I'm looking out over the incredible terraced rice paddies in Sapa and the other spectacular vistas one sees there. We took a horrendous three-hour jeep ride on an almost impassable road to see people from the various hill tribes. On the way back, we had another three-hour trip; it was proven to be worth it when we stopped for a while and explored a marvelous waterfall.

I'll never forget sleeping in a boat in the extraordinarily beautiful Halong Bay, watching the limestone islets fade into the sunset. My wife and I were with a group of some fifteen people taking a three-day tour of the bay. The next day we went to Cat Ba Island. When we were preparing for this tour, we found a bus wasn't available for us. Each of us had to sit on the back of a motorbike to get to the shore, where a boat would take us to a certain part of the island. We were to hike to a restaurant of interest and, for those who were interested, then take a rigorous trek. The path we took to the restaurant was flooded and so for perhaps a half-mile we all waded through about four feet of water, holding our shoes and extra clothes above our heads. The water was fresh and cool and, curiously, that little trek through the flooded path was one of our most memorable experiences.

My mind skips back to Hoi An. I'm thinking about the lovely dinner we had, overlooking the river, the first night we were there. We crossed a little bridge from the main part of Hoi An to get to the restaurant. The waitress brought a fan and turned it on so we'd be comfortable. Then she brought out a series of Hoi An specialties. It was a marvelous evening, sitting there by the river, as the sun set and Hoi An faded into darkness. The next day we had another wonderful meal at a different café overlooking the river, a set-price meal that featured many of the same Hoi An specialties. A man of about forty years old seated us and after we ordered, an elderly woman brought us our first course, which was delicious. "What a wonderful cook she is," I said to my wife, who nodded in agreement. Shortly after this we learned that the woman was a waitress and the man was the cook. Stereotypes die hard.

On each day during our trip in Vietnam we had some kind of wonderful experience—some kind of lovely surprise or unexpected pleasure. I remember seeing hundreds of thousands of storks in the stork sanctuary in the Mekong Delta; the fantastic Cao Dai Cathedral; and having tea with the family of one of our guides in a craft town on the outskirts of Hanoi.

About fifty years ago, I visited the great sculptor Ossip Zadkine. I told him I was about to leave Paris, where I was living at the time, and do a bit of traveling, my version of the grand tour. "You can learn a lot if you keep your eyes open," he said. I think he was right. It's also helpful to think a bit about what you see.

I didn't know what I'd find after I had read the guidebooks and other information on Vietnam. Then I "came and saw," but I didn't conquer. Vietnam conquered me, just as it "conquers" many tourists. I, like many tourists of Vietnam, was "seduced" by this intriguing country.

Chapter 8

Conclusion

THE TOURIST AS STRANGER IN A STRANGE LAND

Tourists, we must remember, are always strangers—people who "drop out" of their traditional pattern of living, generally for a short period of time, and visit a country, especially if it is one that is far away, because, among other things, it is different. It will provide them with new reference points, new ways of living, new experiences, and new challenges.

Ferdinand de Saussure, the Swiss linguist, said that concepts are purely differential and defined negatively—they gain their meaning by being different from other concepts. He also said "in language there are only differences" (1966, p. 118). What he said about the nature of concepts and language also applies to everyday life, to the way we make sense of the world. We are in search of differences, especially when we become tourists, in part because these differences will help us find out who we are. We do this, de Saussure tells us, by finding out who we aren't.

Being a tourist means you must find ways to "make sense" of foreign ways of life and you must be more active in taking care of life's necessities. This experience can be exhilarating—even, I would suggest, for people on organized tours. People on tours still have some time for themselves, generally speaking, and often need to find restaurants, gift shops, and other entertainment.

In addition, tourism has an important educational component. Travel broadens people; they learn that there are other ways to design buildings, cook food, dress, and worship. Until fairly recently, only wealthy people were able to travel and make "grand tours"; the development of mass tourism has changed this.

Many tourists recognize, I would suggest, that travel enables them to transform themselves, often in rather profound ways. They escape, if only for a short while, from their daily routines, their families, their obligations, and the pigeonholes in which they are placed by others. This escape, though momentary, can have remarkable effects on their lives. Just as reading a book or seeing a play can change your life, so can traveling to a foreign country. At its best, tourism is more than entertainment. It is, or can be, a life-affirming experience. I certainly felt that way about my trip to Vietnam.

On the personal level, I should mention that the experience my wife and I had in Vietnam is still the subject of many conversations we have and the wonderful memories we talk about, several years after we flew back to San Francisco from Ho Chi Minh City. The magic of Vietnam lingers. So it should not be a surprise that my wife and I are planning on returning to Vietnam, to stay in Hoi An for a while and then visit some cities between it and Ho Chi Minh City that we missed on our first trip.

A FINAL WORD

In this book, I have offered information about the development of the tourism industry in Vietnam and provided an ethnographic analysis of Vietnamese culture. This analysis is based on preparations I made before going to Vietnam and observations I made while visiting the country. In writing this book, I employed a number of disciplines, such as semiotics and psychoanalytic theory, and I also made use of books and articles by a variety of scholars, travel writers, and commentators on Vietnamese life, history, and culture.

I hope that after reading this book you will not only have learned about the tourism industry in Vietnam but also, as the result of my use of ethnographic methods, that you will have a sense of what it is like to be a tourist there. Countries present themselves to tourists in a number of ways. One important way is through distinctive icons and signs that become lodged in the subconscious minds of tourists as they travel through a country. I have interpreted a number of these signs and icons in an attempt to capture what I have described as the "genius" of Vietnam—the particular quality and character of life lived there as it is experienced by travelers and tourists.

Bibliography

Apple, R.W. (2003). "Looking Up an Old Love on the Streets of Vietnam." *The New York Times,* August 13, pp. D1, D5.

Armstrong, David (2001). "Good Morning, Hanoi." *San Francisco Chronicle,* August 5, p. T1.

Barthes, Roland (1972). *Mythologies.* Annette Lavers, trans. New York: Hill and Wang.

Barthes, Roland (1982). *Empire of Signs.* Rich Howard, trans. New York: Hill and Wang.

Berger, Arthur Asa (Ed.) (1989). *Political Culture and Public Opinion.* New Brunswick, NJ: Transaction Publishers.

Berger, Arthur Asa (1997). *Bloom's Morning: Coffee, Comforters and the Secret Meaning of Everyday Life.* Boulder, CO: Westview.

Berger, Arthur Asa (1997). *Postmortem for a Postmodernist.* Walnut Creek, CA: AltaMira Press.

Berger, Arthur Asa (2004). *Deconstructing Travel: Cultural Perspectives on Tourism.* Walnut Creek, CA: AltaMira Press.

Brownmiller, Susan (1994). *Seeing Vietnam: Encounters of the Road and Heart.* New York: HarperCollins.

CNN (1996). Vo Nguyen Giap [interview]. Available at <http://www.cnn.com/SPECIALS/cold.war/episodes/11/interviews/giap/>. Also available from the National Security Archive, The George Washington University, Washington, DC.

Colet, John and Joshua Eliot (1999). *Footprint Vietnam Handbook* (Second Edition). Bath, England: Footprint Handbooks.

Colet, John and Joshua Eliot (2002). *Footprint Vietnam Handbook* (Third Edition). Bath, England: Footprint Handbooks.

de Saussure, Ferdinand (1966). *Course in General Linguistics.* Wade Baskin, trans. New York: McGraw-Hill.

Dichter, Ernest (2002). *The Strategy of Desire.* New Brunswick, NJ: Transaction Publishers.

Dodd, Jan and Mark Lewis (2000). *The Rough Guide to Vietnam* (Third Edition). London: Rough Guides.

Douglas, Mary (1997). "In defense of shopping." In Pasi Falk and Colin Campbell, eds., *The Shopping Experience.* London: Sage Publications.

Ellis, Claire (2000). *Culture Shock! Vietnam. A Guide to Customs and Etiquette.* Portland, OR: Graphic Arts Center Publishing Company.

Falk, Pasi and Colin Campbell (Eds.) (1997). *The Shopping Experience.* London: Sage Publications.

Flinn, John (2003). "On the level, travel icon Leaning Tower is still full-tilt fun." *San Francisco Chronicle,* October 19, p. C3.

Florence, Mason and Robert Storey (1999). *Lonely Planet Vietnam* (Fifth Edition). Victoria, Australia: Lonely Planet.

Florence, Mason and Virginia Jealous (2003). *Lonely Planet Vietnam* (Seventh Edition). Victoria, Australia: Lonely Planet.

French, Howard W. (2001). "An expatriate who can't resist telling his Mount Fuji story again: Donald Richie offers a collection of his writings on Japan." *The New York Times,* August 8, p. B6.

Fussell, Paul (Ed.) (1987). *The Norton Book of Travel.* New York: W.W. Norton.

Iyer, Pico (1993). *Falling Off the Map: Some Lonely Places of the World.* New York: Vintage.

Leed, Eric J. (1991). *The Mind of the Traveler: From Gilgamesh to Global Tourism.* New York: Basic Books.

Lévi-Strauss, Claude (1970). *Tristes Tropiques: An anthropological study of primitive societies in Brazil.* New York: Atheneum.

Kissinger, Henry (1969). *American Foreign Policy: Three Essays.* New York: W.W. Norton.

MacCannell, Dean (1976). *The Tourist: A New Theory of the Leisure Class.* New York: Schocken Books.

Malinowski, Bronislaw (1961). *Argonauts of the Western Pacific.* New York: E.P. Dutton.

Mok, Connie and Terry Lam (1998). "Hotel and Tourism Development in Vietnam." *The Journal of Travel & Tourism Marketing,* <http://www.hotel-online.com/Trends/JournalTravelTourismMarketing/HotelDevelopmentVietnam_Nov1997.html>.

Pham, Andrew X. (1999). *Catfish and Mandala: A Two-Wheeled Voyage Through the Landscape and Memory of Vietnam.* New York: Farrar, Straus and Giroux.

RailRiders. <http://www.railriders.com>.

Salisbury, Harrison (1967). *Behind the Lines: Hanoi.* New York: Harper and Row.

Thompson, Michael, Richard Ellis, and Aaron Wildavsky (1990). *Cultural Theory.* Boulder, CO: Westview Press.

Urry, John (1990). *The Tourist Gaze.* Thousand Oaks, CA: Sage Publications.

Urry, John (2001). "Globalizing the Tourist Gaze," published by the Department of Sociology, Lancaster University at <http://www.comp.lancs.ac.uk/sociology/soc079ju.html>.

Index

THE HAWORTH HOSPITALITY PRESS®
Hospitality, Travel, and Tourism
K. S. Chon, PhD, Editor-in-Chief

COMMUNITY DESTINATION MANAGEMENT IN DEVELOPING ECONO-MIES edited by Walter Jamieson. (2006).

MANAGING SUSTAINABLE TOURISM: A LEGACY FOR THE FUTURE by David L. Edgell Sr. (2006).

CASINO INDSUTRY IN ASIA-PACIFIC: DEVELOPMENT, OPERATION, AND IMPACT edited by Cathy H.C. Hsu. (2006).

THE GROWTH STRATEGIES OF HOTEL CHAINS: BEST BUSINESS PRAC-TICES BY LEADING COMPANIES by Onofre Martorell Cunill. (2005).

HANDBOOK FOR DISTANCE LEARNING IN TOURISM by Gary Williams. (2005). "This is an important book for a variety of audiences. As a resource for educational designers (and their managers) in particular, it is invaluable. The book is easy to read, and is full of practical information that can be logically applied in the design and development of flexible learning resources." *Louise Berg, MA, DipED, Lecturer in Education, Charles Sturt University, Australia*

VIETNAM TOURISM by Arthur Asa Berger. (2005). "Fresh and innovative.... Drawing upon Professor Berger's background and experience in cultural studies, this book offers an imaginative and personal portrayal of Vietnam as a tourism destination.... A very welcome addition to the field of destination studies." *Professor Brian King, PhD, Head, School of Hospitality, Tourism & Marketing, Victoria University, Australia*

TOURISM AND HOTEL DEVELOPMENT IN CHINA: FROM POLITICAL TO ECONOMIC SUCCESS by Hanqin Qiu Zhang, Ray Pine, and Terry Lam. (2005). "This is one of the most comprehensive books on China tourism and hotel development. It is one of the best textbooks for educators, students, practitioners, and investors who are interested in china tourism and hotel industry. Readers will experience vast, diversified, and past and current issues that affect every educator, student, practitioner, and investor in China tourism and hotel globally in an instant." *Hailin Qu, PhD, Full Professor and William E. Davis Distinguished Chair, School of Hotel & Restaurant Administration, Oklahoma State University*

THE TOURISM AND LEISURE INDUSTRY: SHAPING THE FUTURE edited by Klaus Weiermair and Christine Mathies. (2004). "If you need or want to know about the impact of globalization, the impact of technology, societal forces of change, the experience economy, adaptive technologies, environmental changes, or the new trend of slow tourism, you need this book. *The Tourism and Leisure Industry* contains a great mix of research and practical information." *Charles R. Goeldner, PhD, Professor Emeritus of Marketing and Tourism, Leeds School of Business, University of Colorado*

OCEAN TRAVEL AND CRUISING: A CULTURAL ANALYSIS by Arthur Asa Berger. (2004). "Dr. Berger presents an interdisciplinary discussion of the cruise industry for the thinking person. This is an enjoyable social psychology travel guide with a little business management thrown in. A great book for the curious to read a week before embarking on a first cruise or for the frequent cruiser to gain a broader insight into exactly what a cruise experience represents." *Carl Braunlich, DBA, Associate Professor, Department of Hospitality and Tourism Management, Purdue University, West Lafayette, Indiana*

STANDING THE HEAT: ENSURING CURRICULUM QUALITY IN CULINARY ARTS AND GASTRONOMY by Joseph A. Hegarty. (2003). "This text provides the genesis of a well-researched, thoughtful, rigorous, and sound theoretical framework for the enlargement and expansion of higher education programs in culinary arts and gastronomy." *John M. Antun, PhD, Founding Director, National Restaurant Institute, School of Hotel, Restaurant, and Tourism Management, University of South Carolina*

SEX AND TOURISM: JOURNEYS OF ROMANCE, LOVE, AND LUST edited by Thomas G. Bauer and Bob McKercher. (2003). "Anyone interested in or concerned about the impact of tourism on society and particularly in the developing world, should read this book. It explores a subject that has long remained ignored, almost a taboo area for many governments, institutions, and organizations. It demonstrates that the stereotyping of 'sex tourism' is too simple and travel and sex have many manifestations. The book follows its theme in an innovative and original way." *Carson L. Jenkins, PhD, Professor of International Tourism, University of Strathclyde, Glasgow, Scotland*

CONVENTION TOURISM: INTERNATIONAL RESEARCH AND INDUSTRY PERSPECTIVES edited by Karin Weber and Kye-Sung Chon. (2002). "This comprehensive book is truly global in its perspective. The text points out areas of needed research—a great starting point for graduate students, university faculty, and industry professionals alike. While the focus is mainly academic, there is a lot of meat for this burgeoning industry to chew on as well." *Patti J. Shock, CPCE, Professor and Department Chair, Tourism and Convention Administration, Harrah College of Hotel Administration, University of Nevada–Las Vegas*

CULTURAL TOURISM: THE PARTNERSHIP BETWEEN TOURISM AND CULTURAL HERITAGE MANAGEMENT by Bob McKercher and Hilary du Cros. (2002). "The book brings together concepts, perspectives, and practicalities that must be understood by both cultural heritage and tourism managers, and as such is a must-read for both." *Hisashi B. Sugaya, AICP, Former Chair, International Council of Monuments and Sites, International Scientific Committee on Cultural Tourism; Former Executive Director, Pacific Asia Travel Association Foundation, San Francisco, CA*

TOURISM IN THE ANTARCTIC: OPPORTUNITIES, CONSTRAINTS, AND FUTURE PROSPECTS by Thomas G. Bauer. (2001). "Thomas Bauer presents a wealth of detailed information on the challenges and opportunities facing tourism operators in this last great tourism frontier." *David Mercer, PhD, Associate Professor, School of Geography & Environmental Science, Monash University, Melbourne, Australia*

SERVICE QUALITY MANAGEMENT IN HOSPITALITY, TOURISM, AND LEISURE edited by Jay Kandampully, Connie Mok, and Beverley Sparks. (2001). "A must-read. . . . a treasure. . . . pulls together the work of scholars across the globe, giving you access to new ideas, international research, and industry examples from around the world." *John Bowen, Professor and Director of Graduate Studies, William F. Harrah College of Hotel Administration, University of Nevada, Las Vegas*

TOURISM IN SOUTHEAST ASIA: A NEW DIRECTION edited by K. S. (Kaye) Chon. (2000). "Presents a wide array of very topical discussions on the specific challenges facing the tourism industry in Southeast Asia. A great resource for both scholars and practitioners." *Dr. Hubert B. Van Hoof, Assistant Dean/Associate Professor, School of Hotel and Restaurant Management, Northern Arizona University*

THE PRACTICE OF GRADUATE RESEARCH IN HOSPITALITY AND TOURISM edited by K. S. Chon. (1999). "An excellent reference source for students pursuing graduate degrees in hospitality and tourism." *Connie Mok, PhD, CHE, Associate Professor, Conrad N. Hilton College of Hotel and Restaurant Management, University of Houston, Texas*

THE INTERNATIONAL HOSPITALITY MANAGEMENT BUSINESS: MANAGEMENT AND OPERATIONS by Larry Yu. (1999). "The abundant real-world examples and cases provided in the text enable readers to understand the most up-to-date developments in international hospitality business." *Zheng Gu, PhD, Associate Professor, College of Hotel Administration, University of Nevada, Las Vegas*

CONSUMER BEHAVIOR IN TRAVEL AND TOURISM by Abraham Pizam and Yoel Mansfeld. (1999). "A must for anyone who wants to take advantage of new global opportunities in this growing industry." *Bonnie J. Knutson, PhD, School of Hospitality Business, Michigan State University*

LEGALIZED CASINO GAMING IN THE UNITED STATES: THE ECONOMIC AND SOCIAL IMPACT edited by Cathy H. C. Hsu. (1999). "Brings a fresh new look at one of the areas in tourism that has not yet received careful and serious consideration in the past." *Muzaffer Uysal, PhD, Professor of Tourism Research, Virginia Polytechnic Institute and State University, Blacksburg*

HOSPITALITY MANAGEMENT EDUCATION edited by Clayton W. Barrows and Robert H. Bosselman. (1999). "Takes the mystery out of how hospitality management education programs function and serves as an excellent resource for individuals interested in pursuing the field." *Joe Perdue, CCM, CHE, Director, Executive Masters Program, College of Hotel Administration, University of Nevada, Las Vegas*

MARKETING YOUR CITY, U.S.A.: A GUIDE TO DEVELOPING A STRATEGIC TOURISM MARKETING PLAN by Ronald A. Nykiel and Elizabeth Jascolt. (1998). "An excellent guide for anyone involved in the planning and marketing of cities and regions. . . . A terrific job of synthesizing an otherwise complex procedure." *James C. Maken, PhD, Associate Professor, Babcock Graduate School of Management, Wake Forest University, Winston-Salem, North Carolina*

Order a copy of this book with this form or online at:
http://www.haworthpress.com/store/product.asp?sku=5275

VIETNAM TOURISM

_____in hardbound at $34.95 (ISBN: 0-7890-2570-1)

_____in softbound at $24.95 (ISBN: 0-7890-2571-X)

Or order online and use special offer code HEC25 in the shopping cart.

COST OF BOOKS_____

☐ **BILL ME LATER:** (Bill-me option is good on US/Canada/Mexico orders only; not good to jobbers, wholesalers, or subscription agencies.)

☐ Check here if billing address is different from shipping address and attach purchase order and billing address information.

POSTAGE & HANDLING_____
(US: $4.00 for first book & $1.50 for each additional book)
(Outside US: $5.00 for first book & $2.00 for each additional book)

Signature_____

SUBTOTAL_____

☐ **PAYMENT ENCLOSED: $**_____

IN CANADA: ADD 7% GST_____

☐ **PLEASE CHARGE TO MY CREDIT CARD.**

STATE TAX_____
(NJ, NY, OH, MN, CA, IL, IN, PA, & SD residents, add appropriate local sales tax)

☐ Visa ☐ MasterCard ☐ AmEx ☐ Discover
☐ Diner's Club ☐ Eurocard ☐ JCB

Account # _____

FINAL TOTAL_____
(If paying in Canadian funds, convert using the current exchange rate, UNESCO coupons welcome)

Exp. Date_____

Signature_____

Prices in US dollars and subject to change without notice.

NAME_____

INSTITUTION_____

ADDRESS_____

CITY_____

STATE/ZIP_____

COUNTRY_____ COUNTY (NY residents only)_____

TEL_____ FAX_____

E-MAIL_____

May we use your e-mail address for confirmations and other types of information? ☐ Yes ☐ No
We appreciate receiving your e-mail address and fax number. Haworth would like to e-mail or fax special discount offers to you, as a preferred customer. **We will never share, rent, or exchange your e-mail address or fax number.** We regard such actions as an invasion of your privacy.

Order From Your Local Bookstore or Directly From
The Haworth Press, Inc.
10 Alice Street, Binghamton, New York 13904-1580 • USA
TELEPHONE: 1-800-HAWORTH (1-800-429-6784) / Outside US/Canada: (607) 722-5857
FAX: 1-800-895-0582 / Outside US/Canada: (607) 771-0012
E-mail to: orders@haworthpress.com

For orders outside US and Canada, you may wish to order through your local
sales representative, distributor, or bookseller.
For information, see http://haworthpress.com/distributors

(Discounts are available for individual orders in US and Canada only, not booksellers/distributors.)

PLEASE PHOTOCOPY THIS FORM FOR YOUR PERSONAL USE.
http://www.HaworthPress.com   BOF04